The
WOOD
CARVER'S
DOZEN

The
WOOD
CARVER'S
DOZEN

A COLLECTION OF 12 BEAUTIFUL
PROJECTS FOR COMPLETE BEGINNERS

CELINA MUIRE

QUARTO PRESS

Inspiring | Educating | Creating | Entertaining

Brimming with creative inspiration, how-to projects, and useful information to enrich your everyday life, Quarto Knows is a favourite destination for those pursuing their interests and passions. Visit our site and dig deeper with our books into your area of interest: Quarto Creates, Quarto Cooks, Quarto Homes, Quarto Lives, Quarto Drives, Quarto Explores, Quarto Gifts, or Quarto Kids.

First Published in 2017 by Quarto Press,
an imprint of The Quarto Group.
The Old Brewery, 6 Blundell Street,
London N7 9BH, United Kingdom.
T (0)20 7700 6700 **F** (0)20 7700 8066
www.QuartoKnows.com

ISBN 978-0-85762-188-7

QUAR WCDZ

Editor: Michelle Pickering
Designer: Megan Van Staden
Step-by-step and author photographers:
Celina Muire and Ryan Rose
Studio photographers: Simon Pask
and Phil Wilkins
Illustrator: Kuo Kang Chen
Editorial assistant: Danielle Watt
Art director: Caroline Guest
Creative director: Moira Clinch
Publisher: Samantha Warrington

Printed in China

Note: Woodworking can be dangerous. Both hand and power tools can cause serious injury. Always exercise extreme caution. Always read the instruction manuals supplied with your equipment and use the safety guards provided. All statements, information and advice on methods and techniques given in this book are believed to be true and accurate. However, neither the author nor the publisher can accept any legal liability for errors or omissions.

CONTENTS

—

MEET CELINA

Hello! My name is Celina Muire and I'm a self-taught woodworker. Based in a humble studio in Austin, Texas, I craft a variety of home wares using beautiful hardwoods and locally sourced reclaimed wood. I run an online store selling a wide range of products, from wall art to wooden spoons to bed frames.

As an inherently ambitious and creative individual, I have used a number of mediums in the past. I worked with a variety of materials and techniques, ranging from leatherwork to painting and illustrating, but these pursuits did not bear fruit or retain my interest. A few years ago, I began an exhaustive quest to find a medium I could fall in love with. I was living in a small apartment in Austin, Texas, when I discovered the joy of working with wood, and I soon began dreaming of the day when I could have my own workshop and the freedom to use large power tools without my neighbour's behest for peace and quiet. I took up pyrography (wood burning) for the time being, because it was a great way to get to know the material without the use of large, noisy tools.

When I moved into a house equipped with a small studio, I began to build up my workshop in a feverish haste. However, through hours of practice, experimentation and speculation, I realized that I did not actually need every tool on the market; just a few simple tools would be enough to get through my projects. After many weeks of trial and error, trial and error, trial and error, trial and success finally made its debut. My first successful wooden spoon (that did not look like it had been run over by a truck) was my pride and joy. Since then, I have taught woodworking workshops throughout Austin.

Wood is not a material to be mastered overnight; it requires a lot of patience and practice to understand its magnificent capabilities and hindering foibles. I learned that wood is a medium that presents a constant challenge; a fussy process, but nonetheless a beautiful phenomenon. Woodworking is an equally rich and rewarding creative outlet.

The world of woodworking is extensive, complex and often labour-intensive, encompassing hundreds of tools and thousands of methods. There are many smaller branches of woodworking embedded in the larger, compound mosaic of woodcraft, including wood turning, marquetry, pyrography, bushcraft and wood carving. Due to the unpredictability of the material, the rudimentary craft of wood carving can be difficult at times, but it is a rewarding and practical art. I have written this book to serve as a guide to help novice wood carvers embarking on this exciting skill.

In this book you will be introduced to the basics of wood carving through a variety of beginner tutorials. Not everyone creates quality wood pieces right off the bat; it takes a lot of practice to hone this skill. Therefore, no work is unblemished; there may be some flaws, but be proud. When you run your hands over a wood carving, you can feel the venerated undertaking and gain the intimacy of someone's craft that you would not find anywhere else.

Woodworking can be demanding, but we must respect the fact that this material has lived far longer on the earth than we have. Remember that your small and delicate wood carvings were once part of a massive beast of a tree, growing wild in earth's landscape. Ultimately, when you come out with a final product that is a combination of manmade design and nature's composition, it is quite the accomplishment - and that is the biggest reward this craft can offer.

This book is a recipe for creating simple projects while learning essential techniques. With a bit of time, a few teaspoons of sweat, copious amounts of grit, a dash of determination and a good sense of humour, you will be able to master a wild element of nature - something only the most patient of wood carvers can call an achievement.

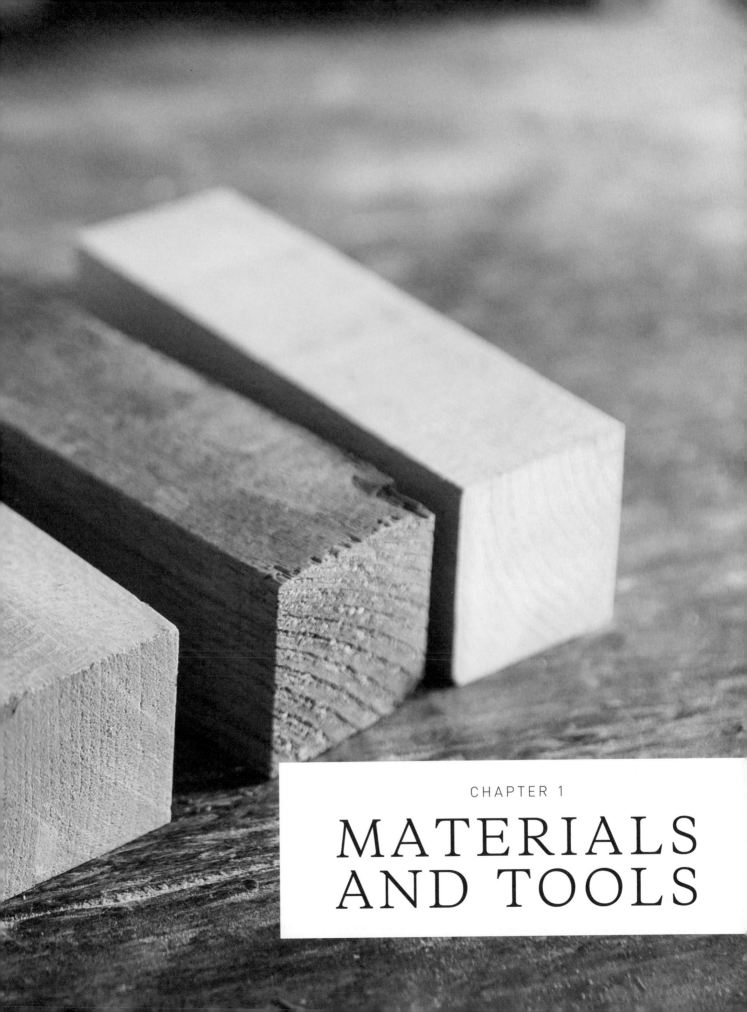

CHAPTER 1

MATERIALS AND TOOLS

TYPES OF WOOD

Woodworkers have a binary catalogue of wood: hardwood and softwood. Although hardwoods are generally tougher than softwoods, the classification is far more complex. Choosing your wood wisely will result in a longer-lasting project.

All trees grow from seeds, and each seed structure either has a covering on it or simply remains naked. Hardwoods are angiosperms (flowering plants) that reproduce with seeds that have some type of exterior shell. Some seeds are hidden within fruit, like the apple tree's; others have a hard covering, like acorns and walnuts. Hardwoods are deciduous trees, which means they shed their leaves annually and have dormant periods. For this reason, hardwoods generally grow more slowly than softwoods, and this slow growth rate fosters denser, harder woods.

Hardwood's dense grain and natural beauty support projects that will often go through a lot of wear and tear. Common uses include kitchen wares (spoons, etc), furniture and flooring.

Softwoods are gymnosperms - a fancy title for evergreens. Think of softwood as hardwood's lofty, carefree counterpart. These trees have leaves all year round, and produce bare seeds that can travel with the wind or simply fall to the ground and start producing. The most common type of softwood trees are conifers (like pine and cypress). Softwood trees grow quickly, and account for about 80 per cent of all timber.

Softwoods are commonly used for outdoor structures - cedar, for example, has great resistance to natural elements and is used for decks. Softwoods are suitable for fine detail carving, making them popular for decorative works, and they are also excellent for whittling projects.

COMMON HARDWOODS

- Ash
- Beech
- Birch
- Cherry
- Mahogany
- Maple
- Oak
- Pecan
- Sycamore
- Teak
- Walnut

COMMON SOFTWOODS

- Cedar
- Douglas fir
- Pine
- Spruce
- Western hemlock
- Yew

CHOOSING WOOD

The woods listed on the next few pages are some of my favourite woods to work with and have been used to make the projects in this book, but they are just a small sample of the wide range available to the carver. You will inevitably discover your own favourites as you try different woods.

When choosing wood for a project, think about how the final product will be used. For example, if you plan on making a spoon, cutting board or anything for the kitchen, it is best to use hardwood. If your project will be used outside, consider carving it from a softwood like pine or cedar.

Some dust particles from certain woods (mostly exotic) can be toxic; it is wise to check with your wood supplier beforehand. Personally, I prefer to use hardwoods with unique characteristics and colours. That way, I can use a clear finish to highlight the wood's natural beauty. For purely decorative projects, colour and grain might be governing factors in your choice of wood.

BASSWOOD OR LIME
Tilia spp.

Also known as linden, American basswood
(*T. americana*; pictured above) and
European lime (*T. × europaea*) are perfect
(soft-feeling) hardwoods for beginner wood
carvers. Growing in Eastern North America,
Europe and Asia, the wood has a notable
pale yellow-and-white colour. The grain is
very subtle; you may have to analyse it
closely to identify the direction of the grain.
Overall, it carves like butter and finishes
smooth. It is best finished with a glossy
polyurethane and/or stain. If you plan on
staining the wood, apply one quick coat of
polyurethane beforehand because it can be
very porous. Failing to make a base layer
can result in a streaky stain colour.

WALNUT
Juglans spp.

English walnut (*J. regia*) and American
black walnut (*J. nigra*; pictured above) are
common hardwoods found in Europe and
North America. The colours vary, with dark
chocolate swirls found on wood from the
centre of the tree, and light yellow streaks
on wood from the outer part of the tree.
American walnut is darker and not as hard
as English walnut. Walnut is one of the
more expensive hardwoods, but the natural
beauty of the grain is exceptional. I do not
suggest staining walnut; finishing it with
oil or clear varnish will effectively bring it
out its natural colours.

CLARO WALNUT
Juglans hindsii

Without a doubt my favourite hardwood is claro walnut. This wood is only found in Northern California and Oregon. Claro walnut trees commonly grow at the base of regular walnut trees and are very unusual looking. They form a dark, puffy structure at the base of the regular tree, which makes the tree look like it is wearing a thick black sock. The grain is unlike anything else, with gnarly swirls of brown, violet, yellow and pink. This wood's wild grain and texture can be somewhat difficult to work with, but the finished product is very rewarding to look at. Any burr walnut - a burr is wood formed from the growth of faults, usually at the base of the tree, and basically a mass of small knots - could be used instead. Burr oak (*Quercus* spp.) would be another good substitute.

BUTTERNUT
Juglans cinerea

Butternut is a member of the walnut family that grows in North America and produces a very sweet nut. Although butternut is technically a hardwood, it has a very soft grain and is easy to carve. It has a light brown colour and an easily identifiable grain. It finishes well with a slight sheen. I highly recommend butternut for beginners, because it is one of the few hardwoods that is easy to carve. Jelutong (*Dyera costulata*), which is native to Asia, could be used as an alternative. It does not have a very interesting grain or colour, but is a soft-feeling hardwood suitable for beginner carvers.

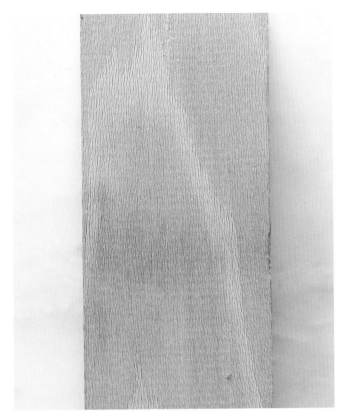

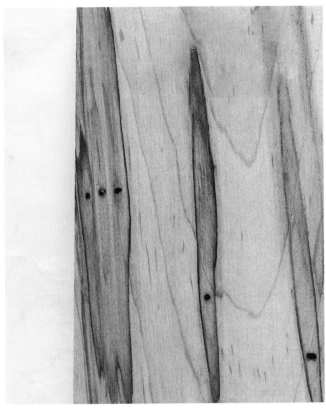

SYCAMORE
Various spp.

Also known as American plane, American sycamore (*Platanus occidentalis*; pictured above) is a hardwood similar to maple that grows in North America. It has a simple pale grain, with notable red specks; I call it the freckled wood. In my experience, this wood is very pleasant to work with and rarely misbehaves. It finishes smoothly and has a fine and even texture. European sycamore (*Acer pseudoplatanus*) is a type of maple and a different species altogether. However, as its Latin name suggests, it is 'like a plane tree'. European sycamore with a plain grain pattern can be substituted for American sycamore; European sycamore with a fiddleback grain pattern is a popular alternative to fiddleback maple (overleaf).

MAPLE AMBROSIA
Acer spp.

This hardwood is by far the most entertaining wood, due to its storytelling abilities that highlight its rich history. The tree itself is actually just a plain maple tree that has been infested with the ambrosia beetle. The beetles bore into the tree, leaving behind tiny holes in the wood, and drag a fungus that discolours the wood and gives it a streaky appearance. No two pieces of maple ambrosia are the same, and we have very talented artists (ambrosia beetles) to thank for that. Like all maple, it finishes smoothly and looks best with a clear coat of oil or varnish. Maple ambrosia is available but not common in Europe, where the discoloration caused by fungus is more widely available in beech; it is called spalted beech.

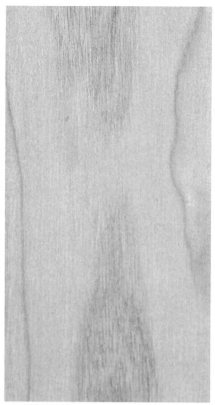

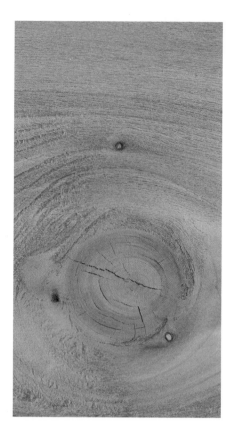

FIDDLEBACK MAPLE
Acer spp.

CHERRY
Prunus spp.

CEDAR
Various spp.

Also known as curly maple, flame maple or tiger maple, fiddleback maple is not actually a species of wood, but rather a maple tree that has a very distinctive grain pattern. Used for the backs of fine violins, it has fascinating ripples that appear when the board is placed in the light, making the wood come alive with movement. The waves have a tiger-stripe appearance and are revealed when the wood is finished and sealed. Like most maples, fiddleback maple finishes well, but can be difficult to use for intricate carving projects due to its wavy grain and texture. European sycamore (*Acer pseudoplatanus*) with a fiddleback grain pattern is also widely used.

Cherry is a strawberry blond hardwood that grows in Europe, North America and Asia. It has a fine, straight grain that makes it easy to work with. It carves and finishes smoothly. When cherry wood is freshly cut, it has a pale, white colour. Over time, it oxidizes as it becomes more exposed to the air, causing it to change to a pinkish red colour. As a result, the cherry tree 'blushes' when it is unveiled in the light. It remains unclear why this wood is so easily embarrassed; its simple grain pattern has a beautiful and classic look. European sweet cherry (*P. avium*) is generally a slightly darker, warmer colour than American black cherry (*P. serotina*; pictured above).

Cedar is a softwood that grows in many parts of the world and encompasses a variety of different species – for example, Eastern redcedar (*Juniperus virginiana*; pictured above), Western redcedar (*Thuja plicata*) and cedar of Lebanon (*Cedrus libani*). Cedar is easy to carve and has a phenomenal, sweet smell when freshly cut. Since cedar has a strong fragrance, it naturally repels insects, making it a fine material to use in the garden. Cedar is lightweight and works well outside in the elements because it is decay-resistant. Colours vary, especially as the wood dries out, from white to creamy yellows, pinks and robust red tones.

TOOLS OF THE TRADE

In the world of woodworking, there are literally thousands of tools with thousands of applications. However, although there are some fundamental tools that are required – chisel, gouge and carving knife – it is not necessary to own every tool that is on the market. The tools used to make the projects in this book have deliberately been kept to a minimum – perfect for beginner wood carvers.

SWEEP NUMBERS

Chisels have a straight cutting edge. Gouges have a curved cutting edge. Both types of tool are numbered according to the curve, or 'sweep', of the cutting edge. Numbering starts at #1, indicating a straight-edged tool with no curvature. The higher the sweep number, the tighter the curve. There are two main numbering systems in use (see right). The tools used in this book follow the Swiss system. Note that the sweep number remains the same whatever the width of the tool.

TOOL	ENGLISH (SHEFFIELD) SYSTEM	SWISS (PFEIL) SYSTEM
Chisel	#1	#1
Skew chisel	#2	#1s
Gouge	#3	#2
Gouge	#4	#3
Gouge	#5	–
Gouge	#6	#5
Gouge	#7	#7
Gouge	#8	#8
Gouge	#9	#9

CHISELS (1)

A chisel is a long tool made from steel that has a sharpened blade at the end with a bevelled tip. The cutting edge may be single-bevelled (bevelled on one side, flat on the other) or double-bevelled (bevelled on both sides). Either type can be used for trimming and shaping the projects in this book, with or without a mallet to suit the specific task.

Bench chisels are multi-use tools that have a basic bevelled tip. They come in a variety of sizes and are designed for general woodworking tasks. Paring chisels are thinner, lighter chisels that are used without a mallet to shave away thin layers of wood. Mortise chisels have a longer, thicker blade and are commonly used with a mallet to chip away a lot of wood in a single pass.

Only one type of chisel has been used to make the projects in this book: a 16mm #1 sweep double-bevel skew chisel. This carving chisel is far less intimidating than its extravagant name implies. It is 16mm wide and has a bevel on both sides of the cutting edge. It is called a skew (or corner) chisel because the end of the blade falls at an angle, instead of flat straight across. The sweep number refers to the curve of the blade; there is no curve, so it has a sweep number of 1 (see above). Personally, I find that this particular chisel works best for the type of projects I make. It is light, goes into the wood easily with a mallet because of the skew and is easy to sharpen.

GOUGES (2)

A gouge is a chisel's curvier friend. Gouges have a curved and bevelled cutting edge at the end of the blade. The varied curves at the cutting edge are specifically designed to make different-size cuts. A gouge is very useful when you need to take away wood in areas where a chisel cannot get the job done. It is also useful for hollowing out the bowl of a spoon. Palm gouges have a small handle that fits comfortably in the palm of the hand and are used when gouging small areas. Gouges with a standard handle can be used with or without a mallet; palm gouges are not used with a mallet.

I use two different gouges in the projects: an 18mm #8 sweep gouge and a ~~5mm #9 sweep palm gouge~~. [handwritten: NOT STRAIGHT AWAY] Sweep numbers range from #1 through #9 (see above). Specialized gouges, such as large U-shaped and V-shaped gouges, have even higher sweep numbers but are not used in this book. Generally, each sweep number can have a tool that varies from 2mm to 40mm in width. Imagine there are dozens of sizes of gouge in each sweep number, and you will start to understand how it would be almost impossible to own every gouge or chisel on the market. This is why it is important to start out with minimal, basic tools to see how you feel about each tool's performance, before going out and investing in the latest, all-inclusive Japanese carving set.

CARVING KNIVES (3)

A carving knife is used for whittling small pieces of wood. The knife's handle is small and the blade extremely sharp. Although carving knives have great technique flexibility, most nicks and cuts come from these tools. It is very important that these knives are used with caution, because the blade can easily slip and nick your skin. Make sure your wood is secured to the table or, if you are working on your lap, carve over a large scrap piece of wood or leather.

Two carving knives are used in the projects: #2 (basic) and #6 chip carving knives, manufactured by Pfeil. (These numbers are specific to the manufacturer.) The basic knife has a 36mm curved blade, with a sharp cutting edge on the inside of the curve. The #6 knife has a 40mm blade with a bevel on one side of the skewed cutting edge. Chip carving simply means wood is being chipped away from a flat surface. These two chip carving knives are great for adding small carving details and shaping the handles of spoons and cutting boards. Generic carving knives are also commonly used for green wood projects.

MALLET (4)

A mallet is used with a gouge or chisel when you need to take out large amounts of wood. The mallet simply applies a stronger force to the blade than your palm. As well as speeding up the removal of large amounts of waste, a mallet can also be invaluable where careful control is required. Although a large proportion of carving is done with two hands on the chisel or gouge - one hand pushing hard, the other restraining and guiding the tool - there are times when it is more effective to tap the tool gently with a mallet. Either a wooden or rubber mallet can be used in conjunction with the carving tools.

SHARPENING STONE (5)

Over time, all carving tools will need maintainance and sharpening. Stones are commonly used to sharpen really dull blades. There are a number of different sharpening stones available in a variety of grits, but almost all stones require lubrication - either oil or water - to keep the surface free from burrs. Burrs develop during the sharpening process, and can prevent smooth contact between the stone and blade.

Beginner wood carvers only need to buy one or two stones. A dual sharpening stone, with a low grit on one side and a higher grit on the other, is very useful. Grading for oil stones is usually simply coarse, medium and fine. A combination oil stone with a coarse or medium grit on one side and a fine grit on the other would be good for a beginner. Water-stone grades can range from around 800 to 8000 grit. A combination water stone with 1000 grit on one side and 4000 grit on the other would be an ideal choice. Tools that go through typical, basic use will not need to be sharpened with a grit below 1000.

LEATHER STROP (6)

A leather strop is very useful for quickly honing tools. The strop is merely a piece of leather glued to wood, with polishing compound (also known as honing, buffing or stropping compound or paste) applied to the leather surface. Tools need to be polished on the strop after sharpening to remove the fine burrs that remain from using the sharpening stone. The strop helps you to achieve a mirror finish. Occasional stropping between projects will help to keep the cutting edge keen.

CLAMPS (7)

A clamp is a reliable, extra set of hands that is used to secure the wood to the table. I recommend that every wood carver should invest in at least two quality clamps. A lot of force can be used behind a carving tool, so it is important to have clamps that are strong and can properly secure the wood.

I used trigger clamps for the projects – either one or two, depending on the size of the wood. These clamps have a quick-release lever for opening the jaw of the clamp, and a squeeze-and-release ratchet action for tightening the clamp in place. They are convenient to use for carving because you may need to reposition and reclamp the wood quite a few times during the course of a project. General-purpose C clamps and F clamps – C- or F-shaped clamps that are tightened with a screw – could be used as well. Sash or bar clamps are handy when you need to glue and secure multiple pieces of wood together. Overall, I find that trigger clamps are the most useful for a variety of projects because they can be the quickest to release and can securely tighten the wood.

DRILL (8)

Drilled holes are required in a couple of projects – for inserting matchstick spikes in the hedgehog tealight holder, and to house the light fitting in the natural wood lamp. In the comb and chain plant holder projects, guide holes are drilled for where you need to carve away the wood with a carving knife or gouge.

RASPS (9)

Although a rasp is only specified in one of the projects (the serving board), this tool can come in handy whenever the grain proves difficult or there is a place on your carving that a carving tool cannot reach. Rasps are made from steel, with small raised cuts on the surface that look very similar to those of a cheese grater. Rifflers can also come in useful; they are similar to rasps but their shape is more unusual, with curved steel on both ends and a handle in the middle. Rasps can take away a decent amount of waste wood, but usually leave the surface very rough, so you will need to follow with sandpaper afterwards.

SAWS (10)

Saws are used in the projects to quickly cut away sections of waste wood that would be too time-consuming, strenuous or difficult to do using carving tools. You will need two types of saw: a handsaw and a jigsaw. The project tutorials always specify which type of saw to use for a particular task – for example, it would be extremely difficult to cut a circle with a handsaw.

It is understood that not all studios/ workshops/living rooms will be able to house large power tools. A giant bandsaw is not required for any of the projects in this book but, if you do have one in your workshop, it will make some tasks a bit easier, such as cutting out the teeth of a comb.

POWER TOOLS

This book concentrates on using hand tools, with the occasional use of a power tool. However, there are times when a power tool makes a job quicker and easier (a power sander, for example), so if you have the tool and the knowledge to use it, I highly recommend that you do so. Remember that power tools tend to make a lot of dust and are very noisy. Power tools can also be dangerous, so it is important to learn how to use them safely and take appropriate precautions.

FINISHING MATERIALS

Perhaps the least glamorous part of wood carving is sanding; all woodworking projects begrudgingly require sandpaper. Once the sanding is complete, though, the fun begins. This may be a rather biased opinion but, for me, finishing any project is by far the most exciting and rewarding part of woodworking. Choosing the right finish can turn any project from a creation into a masterpiece.

SANDPAPER GRADE	GRIT	APPLICATION
Coarse	40 60 80 100	Defining and shaping
Medium	120 150 180	Smoothing the surface
Fine	220 240 320 360 400	Final finishing; sanding between coats of finish

SANDPAPER

Sandpapers are graded by the coarseness of the grit (abrasive particles). The grit is defined on a number scale of 40-400 (or higher). The higher the number, the finer the grit. Numbers can go much higher than 400, but rarely are they needed in a project. Generally, you work through the grades from coarse to medium to fine, until the wood is as smooth as required. Most sanding can start at a coarse grit of 80-100 to remove the majority of the rough surfaces of the wood. After this is done, you can move up to a medium grit of 120-150. Almost all signs of production should disappear at this point. Moving up to a fine grit of 220-400 will finish the job and flatten any grain that remains raised. Most projects can end on 220 grit, but if you want to extend your bragging rights to a super smooth surface, a higher grit can be used. Using a power sander can be really helpful, but it can also generate a lot of dust.

FINISHES

There are a few things to consider when choosing the right finish. Always think about how the piece will be used - indoor, outdoor or on the kitchen table. If the piece will be used in the kitchen, then it will need to be coated with a food-safe finish. That means nontoxic oils and waxes. Common food-safe finishes include beeswax, carnauba wax, mineral oil, shellac, tung oil and walnut oil. My personal favourite is a combination of mineral oil and beeswax.

All other projects can be coloured with a stain if desired, and followed with a protective finish like polyurethane. Common general finishes include lacquer, polyurethane, shellac, teak oil and varnish.

Texas tip: Try to avoid finishing a project when it is humid outside; it will take forever to dry between coats.

CHAPTER 2

TECHNIQUES

PREPARING THE WOOD

———

If you choose the proper wood (hard or soft) and plan out the design by collaborating with the grain of the wood, each project should be a success. Trying to delicately carve an organism that has been growing wild in nature is already a steep undertaking, but applying the following simple procedures can encourage cooperation between your blueprints and wood's naturally complex architecture.

———

IDENTIFYING THE GRAIN

When determining how to set up your project for success, identifying the direction of the wood grain is very important. In order to fully understand why following the grain is so crucial, we must first understand its structure. Trees, like all plants, have a large cellulose structure. Wood is composed of millions of cells held together with a glue-like substance called lignin. Under a microscope, wood looks just like a pair of snakeskin boots - random small, elongated circles bound together in a sea of lignin. The cells themselves are a lot tougher than lignin. When you carve wood in the same direction as the grain, you only split the weaker lignin. When you carve wood against the direction of the grain, you are actually cutting the cellulose fibres as well as the lignin, which can be far more difficult.

POSITIONING YOUR DESIGN

At the mill, the majority of logs are 'plain sawn', meaning the log is sent through the saw many times to cut long, parallel boards. Plain sawing will generally yield the most useable boards from a single log. As such, most boards will have an easily identifiable face grain and end grain. The edge grain merely refers to the left and right sides of the wood.

The ideal, most cooperative face of the wood is the top and bottom of the wood – this is the face grain. The face grain is found on the longest and widest surfaces of the wood – that is our canvas where we sketch out our designs with a pencil. Templates for combs, spoons and other items are drawn on the face grain.

When planning to carve a spoon or something similar with a long thin handle, always sketch out the spoon on the face grain so that the tip of the spoon and the end of the handle run north to south in the same direction as the grain. Avoid placing the sketch going across the face grain. Once carved, the spoon handle can easily snap in half if it does not flow in the same direction as the grain.

The two ends (north and south) of the block of wood will have end grain. It is best to leave these north and south ends alone while cutting or carving until the very end – in other words, do not draw a design on top of end grain and expect to carve it with ease.

———

TRANSFERRING TEMPLATES

Before you begin carving, you must draw your design onto the wood. At the back of this book you will find all the required templates for the projects. Most of these templates are basic outline sketches, and can easily be transferred onto the wood. The templates can simply be torn out and used, but if you would like to reuse the templates or would simply like to keep the book intact (highly suggested), you can grab another piece of paper to trace the original template and use that paper to transfer the image instead.

1 Place the template onto the face grain of the wood. You can tape down a corner to prevent the template from sliding if you wish.

2 Use a pen to draw over the outline, pressing down hard to leave an indention in the wood.

3 Remove the template and use a pen or pencil to trace back over the indented lines on the wood. I recommend that you do not use a marker pen because the ink can easily spread down into the pores of the wood. When you eventually sand down your project, you will have a hard time making the ink disappear.

1

2

3

CLAMPING THE WOOD

When carving with a chisel or gouge, the wood should be securely clamped down flat on your workbench. This is important because a lot of force can be used behind these tools. When cutting out the piece of wood around your drawn design, always try to keep as much wood surface as possible for the clamp. Think of what part of the project you can do first that does not require completely thinning out the shape. A thin piece of wood can be used with clamps, but it will not work as well and will shift throughout the carving process.

A vice is sometimes handy for holding items in an upright position, such as for sanding and sculpting comb teeth. Most (privileged) workbenches have a vice for wood carving, but if yours does not, you can simply secure a scrap piece of wood to the edge of the table with two clamps. Place the carving wood between the table and the scrap wood and tighten the clamps, sandwiching everything securely together.

1 To clamp a piece flat on your workbench, place the top part of the clamp on the piece of wood and secure the bottom part of the clamp underneath the bench. Placement of the clamp can vary; try to have it on a corner or towards one end of the wood instead of centred. You will need room to use the tools and you do not want to be constantly bumping into the clamp.

2 Tighten the clamp so that the wood does not move when you apply pressure to it. For the average project, you may need to reposition and reclamp the wood quite a few times to make sure you are carving from all angles.

3 For projects like spoons that feature a narrow handle, the clamp should go about halfway down the handle. It is important that you do not cut out the entire spoon handle to its proper width before gouging out the bowl. Thinning out the handle first would not be prudent because it may snap from pressure during the gouging process.

1

2

3

BASIC CARVING TECHNIQUES

———

Your mastery of carving techniques will not happen overnight. It takes a lot of practice to form new muscle memory, so do not be discouraged if you find it difficult to use the tools at first. The examples demonstrated here show some general principles for carving with a gouge, a chisel and a carving knife.

———

CARVING WITH A GOUGE

A gouge is one of the easiest tools to use and is very helpful for removing either large or small amounts of wood. It can be used with the hands only or in conjunction with a mallet. Sometimes it can be difficult to carve with a gouge when a surface is completely flat, so you can use a mallet to 'break' the surface – this adds a little more oomph to the gouge cut. Gouges can be used parallel with the direction of the grain, but they also work well for making cross-grain cuts.

USING HANDS ONLY

1 Make sure the wood is secured to the table with a clamp. Grip the gouge with your nondominant hand and place your dominant palm on top of the tool. The bevel (the sloped surface at the end of the blade) should always be facedown onto the wood. Start with the edge of the bevel at about a 45-degree angle on the wood and use your dominant hand to push the tool into the wood with a swift, scooping motion. Use your other hand to control and guide the gouge.

2 The key to using a gouge is to carve away small amounts of wood at a time. Use swift scooping motions to bring up nice clean shavings. Do not try to dig the gouge too deep into the wood because it will result in an uneven and uncontrolled cut.

3 Lift the wood out with the gouge. Shavings should be small and curved. If carving a bowl shape, start at one end of the bowl and then repeat the process from the opposite end.

1

2

3

USING A MALLET

4 To use a mallet with the gouge, hold the gouge handle in your nondominant hand with a loose grip. Hold the mallet with your dominant hand.

5 Tap the mallet on the end of the gouge handle and then lift up the gouge to take out the wood. A simple tap with the mallet will suffice; there is no need to use the arm of Thor. Bring the gouge back up to your starting point, and repeat this technique as often as necessary to remove the depth of wood required.

USING A PALM GOUGE

6 Palm gouges are very useful tools for carving small details. A mallet is not used with a palm gouge. Its handle has a perfect round shape to fit into the palm of your dominant hand. Use this to push the tool and your other hand to guide it.

5

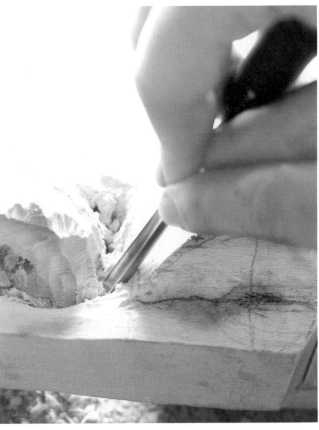

6

CARVING WITH A CHISEL

Chisels are versatile tools that can be used to shave off large chips of wood or thin layers of wood. For the latter, clamp the wood securely, place the chisel against the wood at about a 45-degree angle and use your dominant hand to push the chisel (just as you would do with a gouge) rather than tapping with a mallet.

1 To take out large amounts of wood, secure the wood to the table with a clamp and use a mallet on the end of the chisel. Hold the chisel in your nondominant hand with a loose grip, and place the blade on the corner end grain of the wood. In the example shown opposite (top left), the angle of the chisel on the wood is nearly parallel with the wood block.

2 Placement of the bevel will depend on the type of chisel you are using. If you are using a double-bevel chisel, as featured in all the projects in this book, then there is a bevel on both sides. If you are using a single-bevel chisel (flat on one side, bevel on the other), position the flat side of the chisel against the wood, with the bevel facing up. This allows the wood that is being removed to glide up the bevel towards you.

3 As you tap the handle of the chisel with the mallet, slowly move the chisel into the wood with each tap. Shavings should be long and varying in width.

CARVING WITH A KNIFE

Use a chip carving knife to shape your projects by taking away one thin layer of wood at a time. Carving knives can be used when wood is secured to a table or by simply holding the wood in your hand. Carving knives can be very sharp, so be careful not to nick yourself. If you are working on your lap, carve over a large scrap piece of wood or leather for safety.

1 For small whittling projects, hold the wood piece in your nondominant hand and a basic chip carving knife in the other. Brace your thumb on the wood and use the four fingers to pull the knife towards the thumb in a smooth, shaving motion. The process is very similar to peeling a potato; I have peeled a lot of potatoes in my life, but I find whittling wood with a carving knife to be much more rewarding.

2 The carving knife can also be used without the thumb technique on long, thin pieces of wood, such as spoon handles (see opposite, right). Simply brace the wood with one hand and peel the wood with the carving knife.

3 There are a variety of chip carving knives available, but despite the different blade shapes, most knives use the same technique. To use a #6 chip carving knife with a skew-cut blade, use your forefinger to steady the blade of the knife as you push it into the wood to make a cut, peeling off a thin layer of wood at a time. You can also push the skewed end of the blade down into the wood to cut out recesses in a carving (see opposite, bottom left).

CARVING WITH A CHISEL AND MALLET

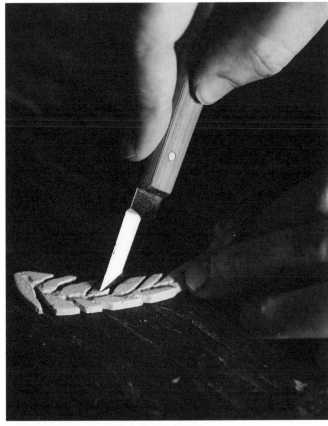

CARVING WITH A #6 CHIP CARVING KNIFE

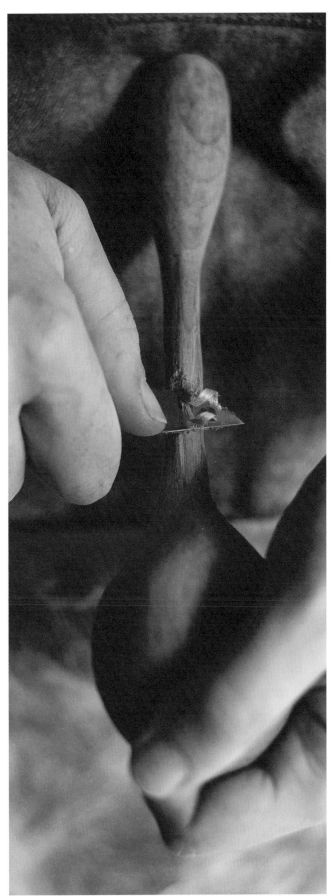

CARVING WITH A BASIC CHIP CARVING KNIFE

SHARPENING YOUR TOOLS

———

From time to time, your cutting tools will need fine-tuning. It is very important to keep your tools sharp in order to avoid injury. More force is required behind a tool that has a dull blade, so it is critical not to overlook sharpening your blades.

———

Having said that, you do not always have to reach for the sharpening stone to fine-tune your tools. Imagine if your mother asked you to clean your room. Usually, your first activity (besides complaining) would not be to vacuum the curtains – that would be a bit excessive. Instead, you would probably make your bed or find some other really simple activity that might mitigate the mess, and subdue the complaints for the time being. Sharpening your tools is just the same. Only break out the sharpening stone after every three to four projects, or when there is a chip in the blade (which rarely happens). Using a leather strop to hone tools is much easier, and cleans up dull blades quickly and efficiently between projects.

SHARPENING A CHISEL OR KNIFE

If using a water stone, as shown opposite, soak it in water for about 10 minutes before use. Maintaining moisture on the stone helps wash away debris from the blade so that it does not impede contact between the stone and the tool. Although this debris (called burrs) can happen on a microscopic level, it is important that it is washed away with water or it can take longer than necessary to sharpen the tool. The following demonstration shows a chisel being sharpened, but the same technique is used for a carving knife.

1 Start with a low-grit stone, like 1000. Find the angle of the bevel on the chisel (about 20 degrees), then drag the chisel back and forth on the stone using a smooth, sweeping motion. Make sure that you maintain the angle of the bevel when sharpening, and concentrate on using the same swift movements to pull the blade in a straight line back and forth. Use light pressure and repeat as many times as necessary.

2 If you are using a double-bevel chisel, simply turn it over and repeat this process. If you are using a single-bevel chisel, the flat side of the chisel will need to be run on the stone in the same fashion. Place the flat side face down on the stone, and rub the flat blade on the stone in a swift back and forth motion. Make sure that the stone is well lubricated throughout, pouring water on the stone as needed.

3 Repeat this process with a finishing grit, like 4000. Analyse both sides of the chisel. Do you see fresh metal on the blade? Are the fresh areas evenly dispersed on the tip of the blade? If so, you can move on to honing the tool on a leather strop.

1

2

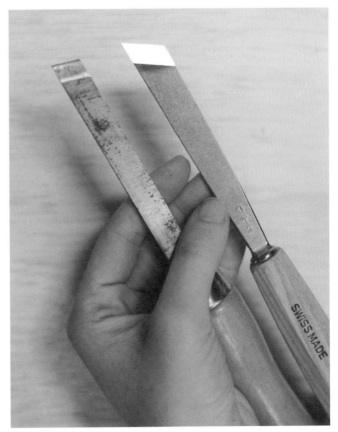

3

SHARPENING A GOUGE

Sharpening a gouge on a water stone uses the same basic principles as sharpening a chisel, but a slightly different technique because of the gouge's curved shape. Start with a low-grit stone (1000) and then repeat the process on a higher grit stone (4000). Use plenty of water to provide enough lubrication so that burrs do not obstruct proper sharpening.

1 Place the bevel of the gouge onto the lubricated stone at about a 20-degree angle. Lightly place your first two fingers near the end of the groove of the gouge. With your two fingers on the gouge and your other hand underneath the handle, move the tool in small, swift circles (or a figure-of-eight shape).

2 Repeat the circles on all sides of the gouge, rolling the bevel on the stone to cover the entire rounded surface. Given its awkward structure, a gouge can be tricky to sharpen. You must pay attention to how many strokes on the stone you are giving each part of the bevel. You may need to stop and analyse the curve of the blade for dull parts on the bevel, and then make sure those come into contact with the stone. After sharpening, all of the dull parts of the blade should disappear.

HONING WITH A LEATHER STROP

After sharpening your tools on a stone, you should then hone them with a leather strop. This will make sure that any remaining burrs are removed, and will produce a mirror finish on the blades. Also use a leather strop between projects to keep tools at their peak performance.

1 To make a leather strop, take a piece of leather at least 5cm (2in) wide and glue it to a piece of scrap wood. Apply some polishing compound to the leather. The compound is made of very fine chemical abrasives mixed with a waxy substance for easy application, and helps to hone and clean the blades of tools.

2 Starting at the far end, draw the tool along the strop towards you at about a 20-degree angle. When you reach the end, lift the tool and start again from the far end of the strop. Do not use the same back and forth movements you used on the sharpening stone; if you do so, you will chop up the leather strop with the crisp blades.

3 Repeat until the blade is clean, shiny and very reflective. Carving knives, gouges and chisels can all be honed on a strop.

1

2

1

2

SANDING AND FINISHING

There are a variety of ways to finish a wood carving, and picking the right kind of finish can be crucial to your project lasting a long time. Sanding the wood piece beforehand is important because it creates a smooth surface so that the finish can be applied evenly across the wood.

SANDING

Sanding is an unfortunate requirement for completed wood carvings. A project is ready to sand when the shape of the project cannot be any more defined with a gouge, knife or chisel. Sanding can result in a lot of dust, so make sure you are in a well-ventilated room before you start.

1 Start with a coarse-grit sandpaper (80 or 100) to define and shape the wood carving. Coarse-grit sandpaper is very abrasive, so try your best to use it in the direction of the grain (although this can be difficult, depending on the project).

2 Move up to a medium grit (120 or 150). This will erase almost all of the scratch marks caused by the coarser grit sandpaper. All signs of use from the carving tools should also disappear. Analyse the piece for any outstanding flaws; it is the job of the medium-grit sandpaper to remove these.

3 When all signs of production have been smoothed, you can move up to a fine grit. Some projects can be completed with 220 grit, but you can move up to 320 grit for a finer finish or even 400 grit if you want to achieve a super smooth finish. Use the fine-grit paper in all directions on the wood. It may be easier to tear or fold the sandpaper into smaller pieces to reach all parts of the carving.

4 You can also fold the paper in half to enable you to apply more pressure to selected areas of the wood carving.

1

3

4

APPLYING A STAIN

If you plan to stain a wood project, do so after you have finished sanding and have removed all dust from the wood's surface. Stains can be used on wood to give it a nice, uniform colour. I do not suggest applying stains on hardwoods simply because of the wood's naturally beautiful colours.

After sanding and removing all dust, apply a thin layer of stain with a foam brush or paintbrush. Brush the stain in the direction of the wood grain. Some people like to use a lint-free cloth to rub some of the colour off the wood shortly after applying it, so that the stain does not fully penetrate into the grain, resulting in a lighter colour. Personally, I do not apply stain that way. If I decide on a stain, I apply at least two or three coats and fully commit to its robust colour. Allow each layer of stain to dry completely before applying another coat. Impatient applications of stain will result in streaky brushstrokes.

Bear in mind that stains do not protect the wood from outside elements; they merely add colour to it. Some stains are premixed with polyurethane. I highly recommend using these mixes because it will save a lot of time; instead of applying a stain and protective finish separately, you can apply them both in one go.

———

PROTECTIVE FINISHES

Both hardwoods and softwoods benefit from some type of protective finish. It can be in the form of a clear varnish, oil, wax or polyurethane. Protective finishes seal the wood and shelter it from hazardous outside elements, such as water, food or dirty hands. A number of projects in this book use polyurethane as a clear protective finish, but it is important to avoid using polyurethane or any other protective varnishes for items that will be used with or around food.

After removing any dust left from sanding, use a foam brush or paintbrush to apply a thin coat of polyurethane to the wood and allow to dry. Apply three or four more coats, allowing each coat to dry before applying the next. For a super glossy look, sand the item with at least 220-grit sandpaper in between coats, remove all dust and then apply the next coat of polyurethane. Apply four or five coats in total to achieve a shiny effect.

SEASONING A FOOD-SAFE ITEM

1 Make sure the item is free of all dust after sanding. You may want to use a lightly dampened paper towel to buff the surface of the wood, making sure the wood is clean and ready to be oiled. Prepare your chosen finish; pictured here is a mix of melted beeswax and mineral oil.

2 Using a lint-free cloth, apply the finish thickly onto the wood carving. Give a generous first coat and allow it to sit for at least an hour to soak into the wood.

3 Return to the wood piece and apply another thick coat of finishing oil. This time let it sit for about 15–20 minutes to soak in.

4 Repeat this process another three or four times to 'season' the item. Since wood has a tendency to dry out over time, you must season the wood properly so that it can be used over and over without drying or cracking.

1

2

FOOD-SAFE FINISHES

Wood projects that will be used in the kitchen require a different finishing process. These items must be treated with food-safe finishing oils or waxes. There are a number of different types of food-safe finish, but one of my favourites is a mix of melted beeswax and mineral oil.

Caring for projects treated with a food-safe finish is minimal. Do not submerge them in water or place in a dishwasher. Instead, wash them with liquid detergent and water. After every dozen or so uses, reapply a food-safe finish to prevent the item from drying out.

CHAPTER 3

KITCHEN
WARES

DESSERT SPOON

—

This is the classic spoon tutorial. There are many variations of the spoon, but this is the basic foundation for carving the bowl and handle.

YOU WILL NEED

Hardwood: approx. 23 × 6cm (9 × 2½in) and 2cm (¾in) thick for one spoon; a 23 × 12.5cm (9 × 5in) piece of maple ambrosia was used here to make three spoons

Pencil

Clamps

#8 sweep gouge, 18mm

#1s sweep double-bevel skew chisel, 16mm

Basic chip carving knife

Bandsaw or jigsaw

Sandpaper: coarse (80-100 grit), medium (120-150 grit) and fine (220-320 grit)

Food-safe finish: mineral oil and beeswax were used here

Lint-free cloth

—

Templates: page 133

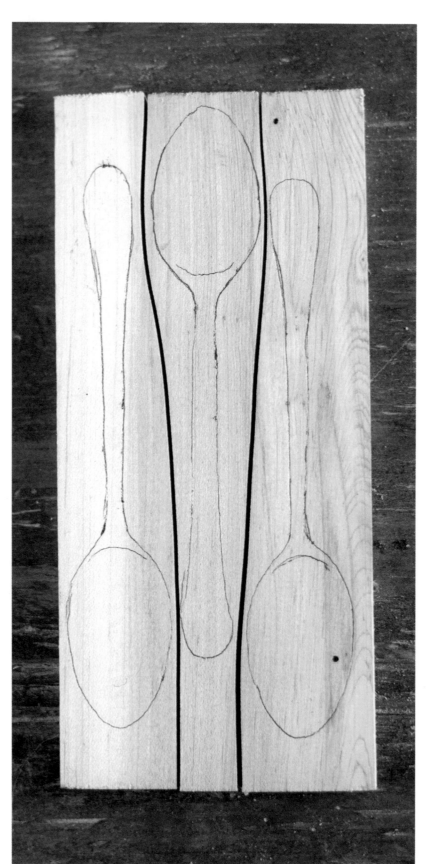

DRAWING THE SHAPE

1 Use the template to sketch the front view of the spoon onto the wood. Position the drawing so that the length of the handle runs in the same direction as the grain of the wood. You can save space on a larger piece of wood by sketching multiple spoons side by side, bowl to handle.

CARVING THE BOWL

2 If you have drawn multiple spoons on a single piece of wood, use a bandsaw or jigsaw to cut the wood into separate pieces for each spoon. Do not cut right up to the outline of the spoons because the extra wood will be needed to support the clamp.

3 Clamp the wood to the table. Use a gouge to scrape out the wood from the bowl of the spoon, starting at the south end of the bowl (nearest the handle). Do the same on the north side of the bowl.

4 Continue gouging a shallow bowl. The bowl of a dessert spoon is not deep; it is deepest by the handle, graduating to a shallow dip at the tip of the spoon. You will know you are finished gouging when you get small, curly chips of wood.

5 Use a bandsaw or jigsaw to cut around the shape of the spoon, but leave extra wood at the end of the handle so you can still clamp the spoon to the table. Use the template to draw the side view of the spoon on each side of the wood. These guidelines indicate how much wood you will need to take away from the back of the spoon.

'This spoon was made with maple ambrosia. Maple is a standard hardwood that can be tough to carve, but is the best long-term, high-use material.'

3

4

5

6

7

6 Clamp the spoon to the table, bowl side down. You may find it helpful to use two clamps on the handle end of the spoon to hold the wood steady for chiselling. Use a chisel to take away the wood on the sides to shape the bottom of the bowl. Start on either the left or right side and push the chisel in the direction of the grain, away from the handle. Only take away small chips at a time. The bowl is fragile in this state and getting too greedy with the chisel can result in a cracked spoon. Be patient or you could end up with a 'spork'.

CARVING THE HANDLE

7 Use the chisel to shape the tip of the bowl and the back of the handle. For the handle, start at the bowl and work towards the tail end to slim down the shape.

8 Use a carving knife to refine the shape of the handle, working from the neck to the end of the handle. Holding the north end of the spoon, lightly carve away the hard edges using a sweeping motion. Don't cut too deeply or you will risk breaking the spoon. Use this technique to round out the curves on the bowl and handle.

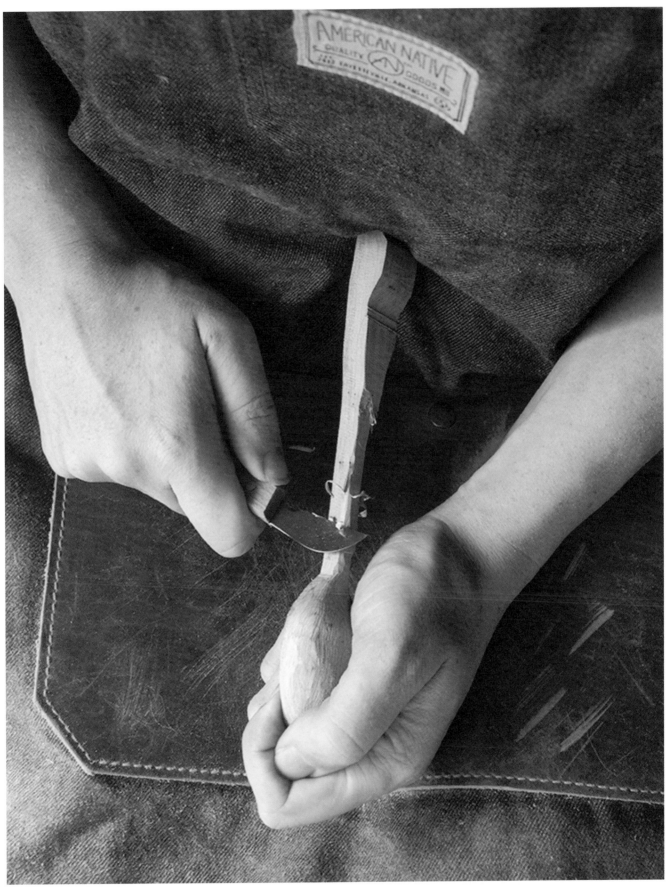

9

SANDING

9 Starting with coarse sandpaper, sand the shape of the spoon. Continue sanding, working your way up through medium to fine sandpaper.

FINISHING

10 Remove all dust from the spoon and apply a food-safe finish with a lint-free cloth. I used a combination of mineral oil and beeswax.

10

SCOOP

—

This project focuses on gouging a deep, even bowl from hardwood.
The scoop has a much larger bowl than its counterpart, the spoon.

YOU WILL NEED

Hardwood: approx. 15 × 15cm (6 × 6in) and 2cm
(¾in) thick; claro walnut was used here

Pencil

Clamps

Mallet

#8 sweep gouge, 18mm

#1s sweep double-bevel skew chisel, 16mm

Basic chip carving knife

Bandsaw or jigsaw

Handsaw

Sandpaper: coarse (80-100 grit), medium
(120-150 grit) and fine (220-320 grit)

Food-safe finish: mineral oil and beeswax were
used here

Lint-free cloth

—

Templates: page 134

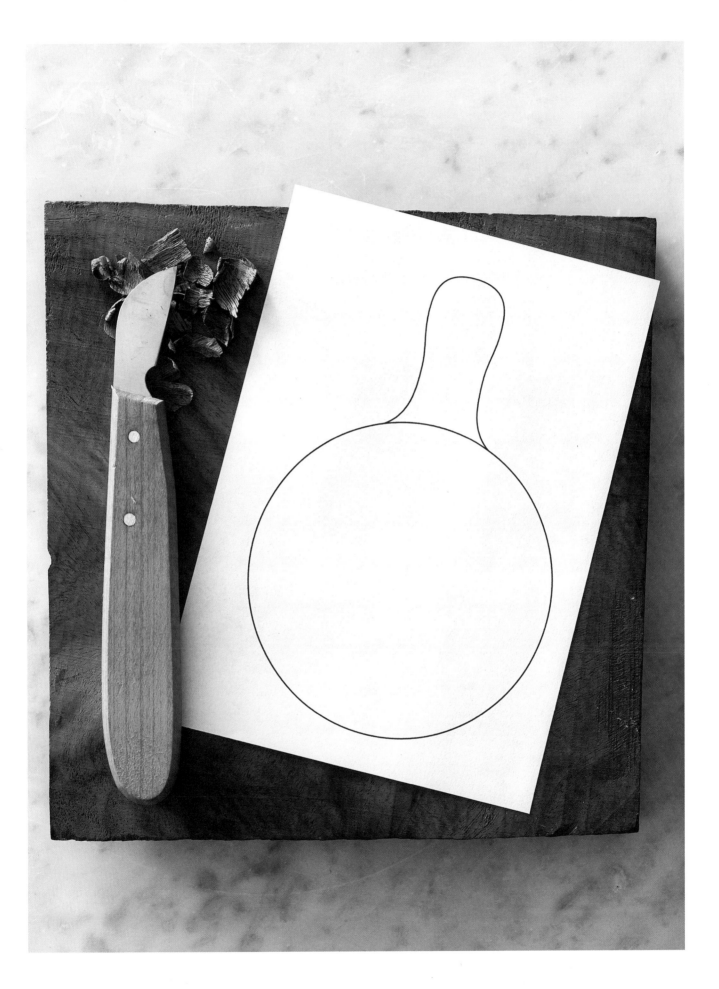

2

DRAWING THE SHAPE

1 Use the template to sketch the front view of the scoop onto the wood. Scoops should have a circular bowl (not oval like a spoon) and a small handle. Position the drawing so that the length of the handle runs in the same direction as the grain of the wood.

CARVING THE INNER BOWL

2 Clamp the wood to the table. Use a gouge and mallet to 'break' the surface of the wood inside the marked circle. Using the mallet lightly, start at either the north or south end of the circle and chip away at the surface with the gouge. Repeat on the opposite side.

3 Once you have created a shallow depression in the surface, use the gouge on its own to scoop away more wood. Start at the outer rim of the circle and gouge inwards. Work systematically around the circle, not taking away too much from one side at a time.

4 Continue to gouge out the bowl of the scoop. Run an index finger inside the bowl to check for discrepancies. Take care not to gouge too deeply or the wood will crack. You will know you have finished gouging the bowl when the chips turn into small curls of wood.

CARVING THE OUTER BOWL

5 Using a bandsaw, jigsaw or handsaw, roughly cut out the circular bowl of the scoop, but do not cut out the handle. Leave a broad area of wood on both sides of the handle; this will provide structural support for finishing the outside of the bowl.

6 Use the template to draw the side view of the scoop on each side of the bowl. It is easy to get carried away when carving the back of the bowl, so it is important to set boundaries to keep the tool from breaking through to the inside of the bowl.

7 Secure the scoop (bowl facedown) to the table by placing the clamp on the handle part of the wood. Use a handsaw at an angle to saw off the north side of the bowl (farthest from the handle). This serves as a shortcut for shaping the back of the bowl.

8 Using a combination of a gouge and chisel, shape the bowl according to the drawn guidelines. Be careful about the direction of the grain because it is very easy to crack the bowl at this stage. This is usually the trickiest part of carving a scoop (or spoon) and the process is a lot slower than gouging the inside of the bowl.

5

6

7

8

9

10

CARVING THE HANDLE

9 Once the inside and outside of the bowl are shaped, use a bandsaw or jigsaw to cut out the rest of the handle.

10 Use a carving knife to shape the handle to your liking. I prefer handles to be slender at the base where they connect to the bowl, and broader at the tip where they will be cupped in the palm of the hand. You can shape the handle differently if you like, or you could go rogue and have no handle at all. It's your scoop; you have that freedom.

SANDING

11 Starting with coarse sandpaper, sand the scoop all over. Move up to medium sandpaper. At this point, most signs of gouging should be sanded away. Finish with fine sandpaper.

FINISHING

12 Remove all dust from the scoop and apply a food-safe finish with a lint-free cloth. I used a combination of mineral oil and beeswax.

11

'This scoop was carved from claro walnut,
which is indigenous to Northern California
and Oregon. Claro walnut grows at the base of
the American walnut tree, and has some really
gnarly and intricate grain patterns.'

SERVING BOARD

—

It is best to use hardwoods for serving boards. This project would also make a great cheese or bread board, but see page 70 for advice on making a more heavy-duty end-grain cutting board.

YOU WILL NEED

Hardwood: three pieces, each approx. 33 × 11.5cm (13 × 4½in) and 2cm (¾in) thick; you can use more or fewer pieces, but they should measure approx. 33cm (13in) square when joined side by side; maple ambrosia was used here

Nonstick paper, such as wax paper, greaseproof paper or baking parchment

Wood glue

2 sash or bar-style clamps for gluing wood together, plus general-purpose clamps for securing the wood to the table while carving

#8 sweep gouge, 18mm

Rasp

Bandsaw or jigsaw

Sandpaper: coarse (80-100 grit), medium (120-150 grit) and fine (220-400 grit)

Food-safe finish: mineral oil and beeswax were used here

Lint-free cloth

'Maple ambrosia is one of the most decorative hardwoods, with distinctive streaks of blue, brown, purple and pink. The ambrosia beetle bores into the wood, making small holes, and carries a fungus that travels through the tree, resulting in unique, colourful streaks.'

2

3

4

PREPARING THE WOOD

1 Since it is very rare that hardwoods come in wide sheets, you will need to assemble narrower pieces of wood together to form a single board of the required dimensions. The three pieces used here will be sufficient to make a serving board about 30cm (12in) in diameter.

2 Protect the table with some nonstick paper. Apply glue along the inside edges of the wood where they will be joined, spreading the glue evenly on the surface. Press the pieces of wood together. Some glue may seep through, but the nonstick paper will prevent the wood from becoming glued to the table.

3 Clamp the three pieces of wood together with a clamp at each side, slowly tightening the clamps all the way. All three boards should lay completely flat. If the outside pieces start to bow up, then you have overtightened the clamps. Wipe away excess glue and allow the wood to dry overnight.

CUTTING THE MAIN SHAPE

4 Draw the shape of your serving board onto the wood. To match the example shown, draw a large circle with a diameter of about 30cm (12in) for the main board, plus a small circle in the corner for a handle.

5 Use a bandsaw or jigsaw to cut out the serving board and handle. (A few different board shapes are shown in the photo.) If you use a jigsaw, make sure the board is securely clamped to the table while cutting.

CARVING

6 Once the basic shape is cut out, clamp the board to the table. Use a sharp gouge to carefully take away the hard edges all around. The chips should be small curls.

7 To make the handle slightly thinner than the main board, use the gouge to shave away a few layers off the surface of the small circle. Turn the board over to the other side and shape the handle and edges to match.

8 Use a rasp to file the hard-to-reach places where the handle meets the main board.

5

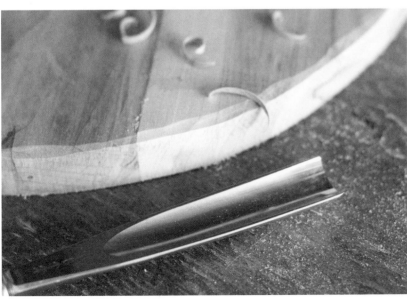

6

8

10

SANDING

9 Use coarse sandpaper to sand the edges and the handle to a soft curve. Continue sanding, working your way up through medium to fine sandpaper. Finish with 400 grit for a really smooth surface.

FINISHING

10 Remove all dust from the board and apply a food-safe finish with a lint-free cloth. I used a combination of mineral oil and beeswax.

END-GRAIN CUTTING BOARDS

The face grain of the wood faces upwards in this project, making it an ideal serving board. Although it is possible to use the face grain of hardwood to make a cutting board, end-grain cutting boards work best and are often used in commercial kitchens. To make an end-grain cutting board, cut numerous small squares of wood and line them up together with the end grain facing upwards. Glue and clamp all the pieces together to make one solid surface. (Note that this brief tutorial may be beyond the scope of a beginner's project.) Chefs love end-grain cutting boards because they extend the life of their knives. When a knife cuts into an end-grain board, the blade slips between the grain of the wood. This helps to keep knives sharp while causing minimal damage to the wood. As a result, end-grain cutting boards can last a really long time.

SALAD SERVERS

———

This simple tutorial shows how to carve a pair of salad servers from hardwood. The bowl of the servers features a 'bear claw' shape, which is an optimal design for grabbing various ingredients in a salad.

YOU WILL NEED

Hardwood: approx. 30 × 12.5cm (12 × 5in) and 1cm (¾in) thick; maple ambrosia was used here

Pencil

Clamps

Mallet

#8 sweep gouge, 18mm

#1s sweep double-bevel skew chisel, 16mm

Bandsaw or jigsaw

Sandpaper: coarse (80-100 grit), medium (120-150 grit) and fine (220-320 grit)

Food-safe finish: mineral oil and beeswax were used here

Lint-free cloth

———

Templates: page 135

1

DRAWING THE SHAPE

1 Use the template to sketch the front view of two salad servers onto the wood. You can save space by sketching them side by side, with the head of each server at opposite ends of the wood. The lengths of the handles should run in the same direction as the grain of the wood.

CARVING THE SERVERS

2 Use a bandsaw or jigsaw to cut out each server. If you are using a jigsaw, make sure the wood is securely clamped to the table.

3 Working on each server in turn, secure the wood to the table with a clamp. Use a gouge to carve a slight depression in the bowl of each server. Maple tends to be very dense, so you may have to 'break' the surface of the wood by using a mallet with the gouge. Once you have made a few initial cuts in the bowl, it will be easier to use the gouge on its own to scoop out the wood.

4 Use the gouge to continue shaping the fronts of the bowls and prongs. The bowls should be shallow, rounding up on the sides and with the deepest dip in the centre, just above the handle.

5 Use the template to draw the side view of each server onto each side of the wood. These guidelines indicate how much wood you will need to take away from the backs of the servers. Clamp the handle of each server to the table, bowl facedown. Using a chisel, carefully round the back edge of the prongs and slim down the neck of each handle where it meets the bowl.

6 Use the chisel to clean up the area where the prongs meet the head of each server. Make sure the chisel is sharp so that it will take away smooth layers. The chips should be thin and curly. The shape of each server should now clearly resemble a 'bear claw'.

2

4

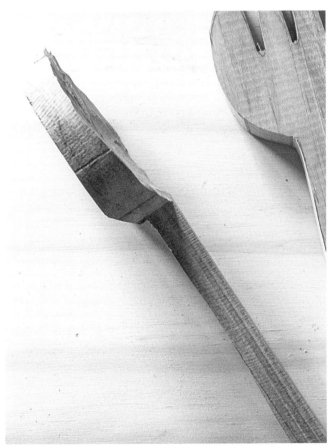

5

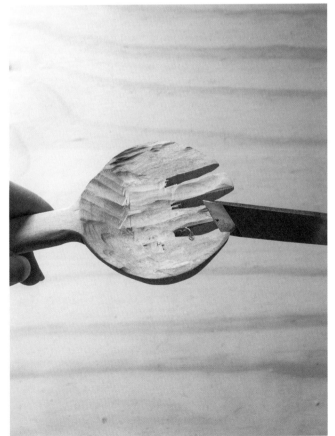

6

SANDING

7 Use coarse sandpaper to smooth out the surfaces of the bowl and handle of each server.

8 Secure the server(s) between your knees (or upright in a vice; see page 116, step 7) and sand each prong. Wrap the sandpaper around the prong while it faces you, and pull the sandpaper from side to side. The grip should be tight enough to cause sufficient friction between the prong and the sandpaper, but not too tight in case the prong snaps. This will slightly curve and smooth the difficult-to-reach areas between the prongs.

9 Continue sanding the server(s), moving up to a medium grit. At this point, all obvious signs of carving should disappear. Sand to a smooth finish with fine sandpaper.

FINISHING

10 Remove all dust from the servers and apply a food-safe finish with a lint-free cloth. I used a combination of mineral oil and beeswax.

9

10

'Maple ambrosia is a fascinating material to work with. No two pieces of this wood are the same, as each tree is unique to the travel patterns of the ambrosia beetles. I used the long length of the server handles to show off the natural beauty of this wood.'

DISH

—

*This project is gouge heavy and involves a lot of hard work.
However, the end result is a beautiful dish, plate or catch-all.*

YOU WILL NEED

Hardwood: approx. 25 × 20cm (10 × 8in) and 2cm
(¾in) thick; fiddleback maple was used here

Pencil

Clamps

Mallet

#8 sweep gouge, 18mm

#1s sweep double-bevel skew chisel, 16mm

Bandsaw or jigsaw

Sandpaper: coarse (80-100 grit), medium
(120-150 grit) and fine (220-400 grit)

Suitable finish: if the dish will be for food,
use a food-safe finish such as mineral oil and
beeswax; otherwise use a finish of your choice
such as polyurethane

Lint-free cloth for oil/wax finish, or foam brush or
paintbrush for polyurethane

2

DRAWING THE SHAPE

1 Draw a circle on the wood; the dish shown is about 18cm (7in) in diameter. Take care to leave enough room outside the circle for clamping the wood to the table while carving.

CARVING THE INNER BOWL

2 Clamp the wood to the table. Use a gouge and mallet to carve out the inside of the bowl, starting at the south end of the circle. Gouge in the direction of the grain and stop when you reach the centre. Repeat at the north end of the circle. Ideally, the wood chips should be long and thin.

3 Continue using the mallet with the gouge until there are roughly straight streaks running in the direction of the grain, from north to south. Essentially, it should look like a circle with a lot of stripes in it.

4 At this point, it should be easier to use the gouge on its own to scoop out the wood. Start from the outside edge on either the north or south ends and work your way towards the centre. Since it is difficult to make deep cuts using the gouge with this motion, you will be required to work at an even pace around the rim, taking away one layer of wood at a time. The chips should now be large curls.

5 By now you should have enough chips on the ground to make a (prickly) rug; you could even save them to stuff an organic mattress, if that's what you're into. Continue gouging from the north and south ends of the circle, using the direction of the grain to your advantage.

6 As the shallow bowl begins to appear, start using the gouge on the east and west sides of the circle. Go slowly towards the centre with the tool. When you gouge against the grain, you can hear how it makes a different noise; it sounds like paper tearing. Run your hand inside the dish to feel for any unevenness.

3

4

5

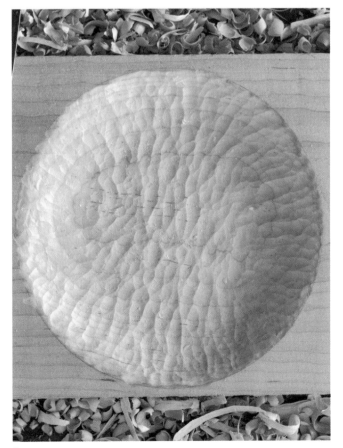

6

7

8

9

CARVING THE OUTER BOWL

7 Use a bandsaw or jigsaw to cut out the gouged circle.

8 Clamp the dish upside down on the table, and gently use a gouge or chisel to remove the wood around the edges to create a soft curve on the underside of the dish.

SANDING

9 Starting with coarse sandpaper, sand the inside and outside of the dish. Continue sanding, working your way up from medium to fine sandpaper. I chose to leave signs of gouging inside the dish, as proof of my hard work – it's a mild trophy to show off to others. Sand up to 400 grit on the outside for a really smooth surface.

FINISHING

10 Remove all dust from the dish. If you plan to use the dish in a food setting, finish with a food-safe finish such as a combination of mineral oil and beeswax. Otherwise, you can apply a couple of coats of polyurethane to protect the wood.

'This project was carved from fiddleback maple. This wood is also known as tiger maple because of the distinct stripes that are revealed when you apply finishing oils to the wood. I think this challenging tutorial takes "earning your stripes" to a whole different level.'

JAM SPREADER

—

This is a great project for using any scraps of wood you might have lying around. The spreader can be used for jam, but also as a cheese knife, pâté knife or butter knife – whatever suits your fancy.

YOU WILL NEED

Hardwood: approx. 20 × 4cm (8 × 1½in) and 13mm (½in) thick for one jam spreader; a 20 × 6cm (8 × 2½in) piece of American walnut was used here to make two jam spreaders

Pencil

Clamps

#8 sweep gouge, 18mm

#1s sweep double-bevel skew chisel, 16mm

Basic chip carving knife

Bandsaw or jigsaw

Sandpaper: coarse (80-100 grit), medium (120-150 grit) and fine (220-320 grit)

Food-safe finish: mineral oil and beeswax were used here

Lint-free cloth

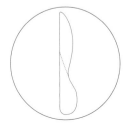

—

Template: page 136

2

DRAWING THE SHAPE

1 Use the template to sketch the shape of the jam spreader onto the wood. Position the drawing so that the length of the spreader runs in the same direction as the grain of the wood. The top edge of the spreader should be the straightest, so align that edge with the straight edge of the wood. You can save space on a piece of wood by sketching two spreaders side by side, aligned along opposite edges of the wood.

CARVING

2 Use a bandsaw or jigsaw to cut out the main shape of the spreader, but don't cut out the middle curve just yet. This extra wood will provide structural support when using a chisel in the next step. Without it, the spreader could snap.

3 Clamp the handle end to the table and use a chisel to shave away the blade. Use one fluid, sweeping motion all the way through to the end of the blade. You should get thin, super curly chips when doing this; if not, it means that your chisel needs sharpening.

4 There should be an obvious curve from handle to blade as the spreader takes shape. Use a gouge to take away small chips of wood to shape this curve further, but make sure you do not carve too much from the centre of the spreader. When you use it, your index finger will put pressure on the middle of the spreader and, if there is not proper support connecting the handle to the blade, the spreader will snap. Continue using the chisel until the blade of the spreader is less than 6mm (¼in) thick. The 'slant' located in the centre of the jam spreader template serves as a guide to show where the most pressure will be placed when in use.

3

4

5

6

5 Use a carving knife to shape the middle curve where the handle and blade meet on the underside of the spreader. Also use the knife to round out the sides of the handle.

SANDING

6 Use coarse sandpaper to shape the jam spreader. Smooth and sharpen the edge of the blade with medium sandpaper. Continue sanding, working up to fine sandpaper.

FINISHING

7 Remove all dust from the wood and apply a food-safe finish with a lint-free cloth. I used a combination of mineral oil and beeswax.

7

—

'The jam spreader in the step-by-step demonstration was carved from American walnut. The other finished examples pictured opposite were made from claro walnut and maple ambrosia.'

EGG HOLDER

—

This project focuses on the art of the gouge. It can be a challenge to make six even bowls in alignment, but this tutorial will help you perfect your carving techniques.

YOU WILL NEED

Hardwood: approx. 20 × 15cm (8 × 6in) and 2.5cm (1in) thick; claro walnut was used here

Pencil

Clamps

Mallet

#8 sweep gouge, 18mm

Sandpaper: coarse (80-100 grit), medium (120-150 grit) and fine (220-320 grit)

Food-safe finish: mineral oil and beeswax were used here

Lint-free cloth

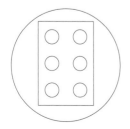

—

Template: page 137

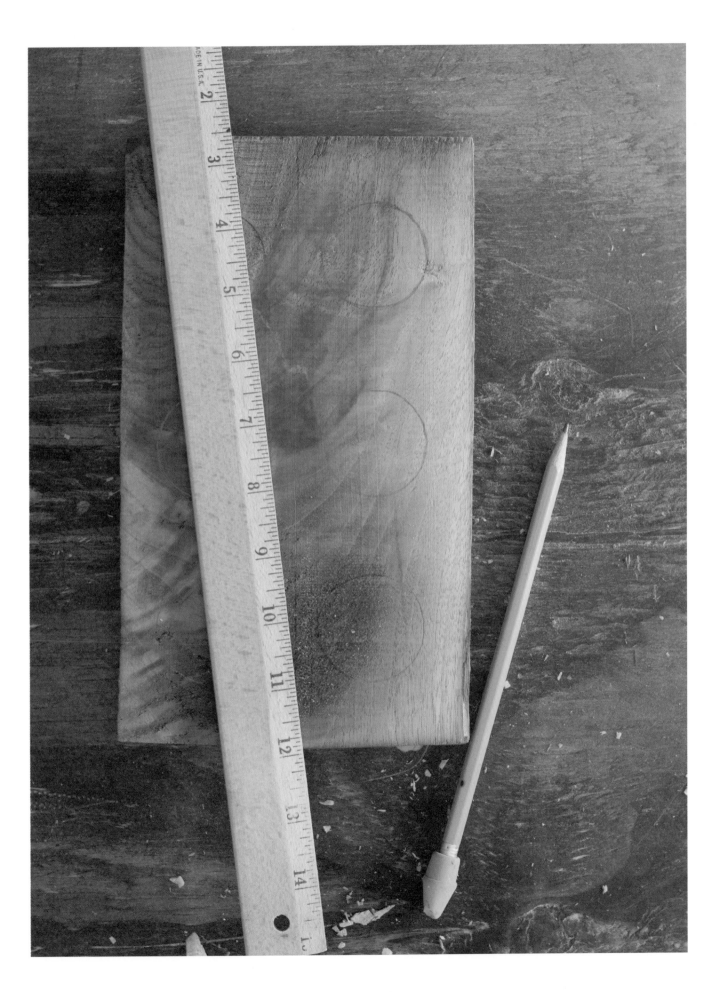

DRAWING THE SHAPE

1 Start with a piece of wood of the required size for your egg holder, and use the template to draw six circles onto the wood. You could use a larger piece of wood and draw a dozen circles if you feel extra ambitious. Make sure to leave about 3cm (1¼in) between the circles.

CARVING

2 Clamp the wood to the table. Use a gouge and mallet to scoop out the surface of the wood from inside each circle. Start at one end of the circle (either the north or south end of the grain pattern) and chip away at the surface. Repeat at the opposite end. The chips should be large and irregular.

3 Once you have created a shallow depression in the surface, use the gouge on its own to scoop away more wood.

4 Work systematically around each circle, gouging from the rim inwards to the centre and not taking away too much from one side at a time. As you get closer to completing each bowl, the chips will become finer and extra curly.

SANDING

5 Starting with coarse sandpaper, sand the inside of each bowl and around the edges of the wooden board. Continue sanding, working your way up through medium to fine sandpaper. I sanded the edges down to a curve to give the egg holder a quasi-professional look.

FINISHING

6 Remove all dust from the wood and apply a food-safe finish with a lint-free cloth (pictured overleaf). I used a combination of mineral oil and beeswax.

2

3

4

5

—

'This egg holder was carved from claro walnut. Check out the amazing grain and colour variation. Claro walnut is my favourite wood. Although the intense grain can be difficult to carve, the end result has beautiful pink, gold, purple and brown swirls. It truly is the Neapolitan of wood.'

6

CHAPTER 4

HOME
WARES

DOG BUSINESS CARD HOLDER

—

This dog is the jack of all trades. Not only does he hold business cards, but photographs and postcards too.

YOU WILL NEED

Softwood or hardwood: 7.5 × 5cm (3 × 2in) and 5cm (2in) thick; butternut was used here

Pencil

Basic chip carving knife

#6 chip carving knife

Bandsaw or handsaw

Sandpaper: coarse (80-100 grit), medium (120-150 grit) and fine (220-320 grit)

Polyurethane (used for sample shown) or finishing oil

Foam brush or paintbrush for polyurethane, or lint-free cloth for finishing oil

—

Templates: page 138

'For this project I used butternut, which is a soft but
durable hardwood. The butternut tree bears fruit
similar to the walnut tree. The wood has a light,
golden brown colour and is easy to carve.'

2

3

4A

4B

DRAWING THE SHAPE

1 Use the templates to sketch the outline of the dog's head onto each face of the wood. Make sure that you draw the correct head profile onto the correct face of the wood – top, bottom and both side views – and in the correct orientation.

CARVING THE HEAD

2 Hold the block of wood in your palm and use a #6 chip carving knife to shape the dog's snout. Chip away each corner of the wood towards the tip of the snout, carving all the way up to the drawn outlines. Do this at all four corners of the snout.

3 Using the snout template as a guide, draw a line across the end of the wood that connects the mouth from the left side of the dog's face to the right side. Draw a circle on the end of the wood to serve as a guide for the thickness of the snout.

4 Use the #6 knife to shave the wood around the snout all the way down to the drawn circle.

5 Use a combination of the #6 knife and a basic chip carving knife to finish carving the dog's head. Carve a space between the top of the ears, and curves for the top of the brow bone. It is important to make sure there is definition in the brow bone and between the ears. Failing to do so may cause your carving to look more like a pig than a canine.

ADDING DETAILS

6 Use a bandsaw or handsaw to slice a cut across the line of the dog's mouth. This will be used for holding business cards and so on, and should be about 13mm (½in) deep and 2–3mm (⅛in) wide.

7 Use the basic chip carving knife to carve the eyes. Referring to the eye template for guidance, start by carving out small chips on the outside corner of each eye, stopping where the eyeball starts. Shave a small incline across the top of the eyeball towards the top lid, then carve out a small chip on the inside corner. Gradually carve away wood underneath the eye. The carving should be deepest in the corners of the eye, so focus on perfecting these aspects of the eyes to achieve a 3D look. When you start sanding the dog, double check the eyes and add further definition with the carving knife if necessary.

SANDING

8 Sand the entire dog to a smooth finish, starting with coarse sandpaper and working your way up through medium to fine sandpaper.

FINISHING

9 Remove all dust from the wood and apply your chosen finish. To match the glossy look of the dog shown here, apply a layer of polyurethane, allow it to dry and then sand the dog again with 320-grit sandpaper. Dust off the dog and apply another thin coat of polyurethane. Repeat this process four or five times to give the dog a smooth, shiny finish.

6

8

9

HEDGEHOG TEALIGHT HOLDER

I think it helps to name your hedgehog when making this project because hedgehogs can be very shy and may need some encouragement to appear. I named this guy Felipe – Pepe for short.

YOU WILL NEED

Softwood or hardwood: 28 × 9cm (11 × 3½in) and 5cm (2in) thick (a shorter piece can be used but it will fit fewer tealights); basswood was used here

Pencil

Clamps

#8 sweep gouge, 18mm

#9 sweep palm gouge, 5mm

Drill and 3mm drill bit

Bandsaw, handsaw or jigsaw

Sandpaper: coarse (80-100 grit), medium (120-150 grit) and fine (220-320 grit)

Polyurethane (used for sample shown) or finishing oil

Foam brush or paintbrush for polyurethane, or lint-free cloth for finishing oil

Matches: 60-70 were used for this hedgehog's spikes

Three tealights

Templates: page 139

2

3

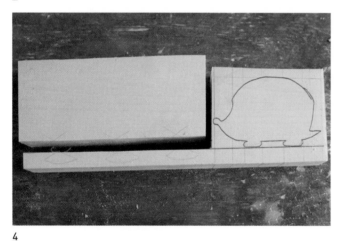

4

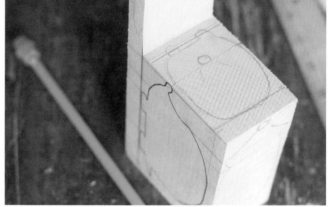

5

DRAWING THE SHAPE

1 Draw a line along the front face of the wood, 13mm (½in) up from the bottom. Use the template to sketch the side view of the hedgehog at one end of the wood, standing on the line and facing inwards. Measure and mark where the three tealights will go for reference.

2 In order to sketch the hedgehog in the correct position on the other faces of the wood, use the hedgehog's identifying features to your advantage. Draw vertical lines at the tip of the nose, brow, front and back of each foot, and tip of the tail. Continue these guidelines around all four faces of the wood.

3 Mark guidelines for the back and tail across the end grain of the wood. Use the templates and guidelines to sketch the top, back and remaining side view of the hedgehog on the wood.

4 Using a bandsaw, handsaw or jigsaw, cut out and discard the rectangular piece of wood above the drawn 13mm (½in) baseline in front of the hedgehog, just before the tip of the nose.

5 Use the template to sketch the front view of the hedgehog on the wood, drawing guidelines to align the nose, feet and top of the hedgehog as before.

6

7

CARVING THE HEDGEHOG

6 Clamp the wood to the table. Starting at the second guideline (marking the brow) on the top face of the wood, use a #8 gouge to chip away the top layer of wood down towards the end of the snout. Don't worry about chipping away the sketch of the hedgehog while you do this; it serves merely as a visual guide. As you progress in this carving, you may need to redraw the sketches or simply refer to them, so keep the templates handy.

7 Moving on to the third guideline (front of first foot), use the gouge to sweep away the wood above the head towards the nose of the hedgehog. As you take out more wood from the top, it becomes easier to go back to the brow guideline and shave off more wood over the snout. Refer to the guidelines on both the left and right sides of the block. Make sure not to carve out any wood below the drawn outlines.

8 Continue moving back along the guidelines, gouging out all wood down to the hedgehog outlines drawn on the left and right sides of the wood. Pay attention to the curve of the back; recognizing how this shape takes form will help with the next step.

8

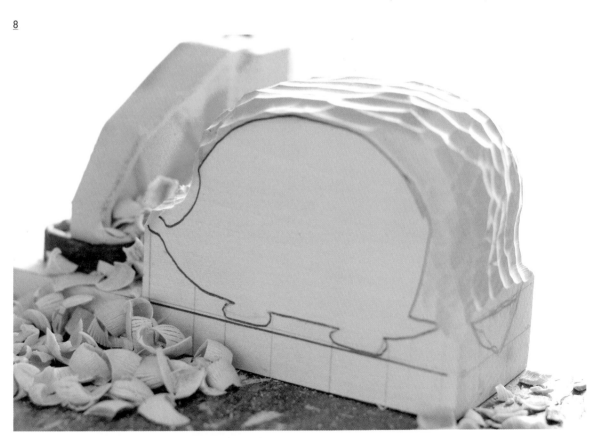

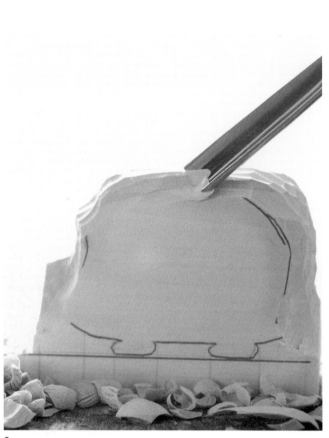

9

10

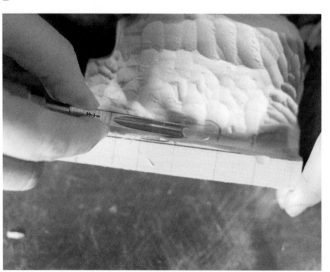

11

9 Now use the gouge to take off the straight side edges around the hedgehog's back. Use soft, sweeping motions, taking only small curly chips away each time. Again, do not worry about the template marks disappearing; the hedgehog will really start to take form at this stage.

10 While the wood is still clamped, use a #9 palm gouge to take away the sides of the wood around the feet area. Remember that hedgehogs have tiny little paws under a big belly, so it is safe to take away quite a bit of wood from the sides.

11 Unclamp the piece and hold it in your lap while using the palm gouge to carefully take out the wood between the front and back feet.

12A

12 A palm gouge is perfect for delicate carving, so use it to take away wood around the face to make the perfect snout. Also use it to perfect the tail on your tiny friend.

12B

13

15

14

back in between the feet. These guidelines will cross at the centre on top of the back. Clamp the wood to the table and use a 3mm bit to drill a hole on this mark, about 2cm (¾in) deep straight down into the hedgehog's back. Insert a matchstick to double check the size of the hole.

15 Drill as many holes for the matches as you wish. This hedgehog has seven rows of holes, with about nine holes in each row. Finish sanding up to 220 grit or more.

FINISHING

16 Remove all dust from the wood and apply your chosen finish. The sample shown has been finished with four or five coats of polyurethane, allowing each coat to dry and sanding lightly with 320-grit sandpaper between coats. If you are also using basswood (or lime) and would like to stain it, apply a coat of polyurethane first. Basswood is very absorbent, so failing to seal the wood with a coat of polyurethane first can result in a streakily coloured hedgehog.

17 Once the piece has dried, insert a matchstick into each hole. If you own 'strike anywhere' matches, you can glue a small piece of sandpaper to the side of the tealight holder. Regular matches will still need the phosphorus striking plate found on the match box. Lay out the tealights on the holder. Make sure you don't place the candles too close to the hedgehog's snout.

SANDING AND DRILLING

13 Sand the entire piece using coarse and then medium sandpaper.

14 Draw a line from the middle of the tail all the way over the back to the snout, and another line running across the centre of the

*'This hedgehog was carved from basswood.
Basswood is a soft but durable hardwood
and one of the easiest to carve. I strongly
recommend this wood for beginners.'*

COMB

—

Wooden combs are not just aesthetic keepsakes.
They are much more gentle than plastic combs, and help
distribute natural oils evenly throughout the hair.

YOU WILL NEED

Hardwood: approx. 9 × 7.5cm (3½ × 3in) and 13mm
(½in) thick; cherry was used here

Pencil

Clamps

#9 sweep palm gouge, 5mm

#6 chip carving knife

Bandsaw or jigsaw

Drill and 3mm drill bit (if you don't have a bandsaw)

Sandpaper: coarse (80-100 grit), medium
(120-150 grit) and fine (220-400 grit)

Polyurethane or finishing oil: mineral oil was used
here, but any type of oil would work well for a
hair comb

Lint-free cloth for finishing oil, or foam brush or
paintbrush for polyurethane

—

Templates: page 140

*'This comb was carved from cherry wood.
Cherry is a relatively easy hardwood to work
with, but it is also durable. Cherry wood often
starts off looking very pale, but over time the
wood oxidizes and ages very well, resulting
in rich brown and red streaks.'*

DRAWING THE SHAPE

1 Use the template to sketch the outline of the comb onto the wood, making sure that the comb teeth run in the same direction as the grain. The width and spacing of the teeth on the template will produce an effective comb, but the design on the handle is optional. Templates for a selection of decorative elements have been provided for the handle. Feel free to create your own design or simply leave the handle plain for a classic look.

3

4

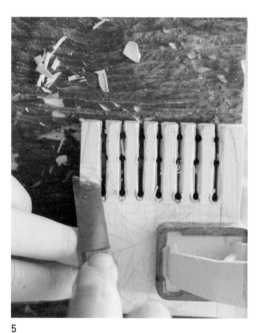

5

CARVING THE TEETH

2 If you have a bandsaw, slowly cut out the wood between the comb teeth. Otherwise, add markings for drilling three guide holes in each space between the comb teeth. Try to align the holes in three rows, at the top, middle and bottom of the spaces. Use a 3mm bit to drill each hole.

3 Use a #6 chip carving knife to chip away the wood between the teeth. Start by driving the blade into the pencil line on one side of the drilled holes and then push inwards towards the centre. Repeat from the pencil line on the other side of the drilled holes.

Don't chip away anything outside of the drilled holes. Carve about halfway through the wood.

4 Flip the comb over and use a pencil to mark guidelines connecting the three holes in each space. Use the carving knife to chip away the wood between the teeth, pushing the knife inwards towards the centre of the drilled holes, until you carve through to the other side of the comb.

5 Clamp the wood flat on the table with the drawn handle design facing upwards. Start at the base of the teeth near the handle, and use the carving knife, bevel up, to gently

6A

shave down the wood along the length of
each tooth. As you work in the direction
of the grain, the shavings should be small
and curly. Take your time carving the teeth,
and don't remove too much wood at one
time or the teeth will surely snap.

6 Use the carving knife with the bevel
touching the tooth to gently chip away the
sides of each tooth. The goal is to take out all
of the wood that shows signs of drilled holes.

6B

7

8

9

SANDING THE TEETH

7 If you have a vice for your workbench, this step will be a breeze; simply secure the handle of the comb in the vice with the teeth extending upwards, ready to sand. If you are working on a normal table, you can rig a simple vice by placing a piece of scrap wood alongside the edge of the table. Place the comb, teeth up, between the scrap wood and the table. Use two clamps to secure the scrap wood to the table, holding the comb firmly in between.

8 Starting with coarse sandpaper, place the paper in one of the spaces between the teeth so that the sandpaper 'hugs' one of the teeth. Stand to the side of the comb and pull the sandpaper towards you with one hand and then the other. Use a rapid, sweeping motion, going from side to side to sand and shape the tooth. Use the same technique for each tooth until all sides of the teeth are sanded. Work your way up to 120–320 grit. The ends of the teeth will start to take a pointy shape. This is a good sign.

CARVING THE HANDLE

9 Depending on your enthusiasm for detail carving, you can leave the handle plain or carve it with a decorative design. Clamp the comb flat on the table and use a palm gouge to carve out the design. This comb has quite a few ambitious layers of carving – I hope yours does too!

10 Use a bandsaw or jigsaw to cut out the top of the handle from the remaining wood. Use sandpaper to round out the top edges.

FINISHING

11 Finish sanding the entire comb with 400-grit sandpaper. Remove all dust from the wood and apply your chosen finish with a lint-free cloth. This comb was finished with mineral oil to show off the natural grain of the cherry wood. You can use other types of finish, but bear in mind that this item will be run through hair, so any type of oil (mineral, grapeseed, etc) should work fine. Try to avoid thick varnishes because they could clog some of the detailed carving.

NATURAL WOOD LAMP

———

*This project is really flexible on the type of wood you can use,
and each lamp will be unique, depending on the shape,
size and colour of the wood you choose.*

YOU WILL NEED

Large piece of wood (soft, hard or green);
green cedar was used here

Pencil

Clamps

Mallet

#8 sweep gouge, 18mm

#1s sweep double-bevel skew chisel, 16mm

Drill and spade bit, at least 25mm wide

Handsaw

Sandpaper: coarse (80-100 grit), medium
(120-150 grit) and fine (220-400 grit)

Polyurethane or finishing oil: teak oil was used here

Lint-free cloth for finishing oil, or foam brush or
paintbrush for polyurethane

Lamp kit consisting of socket, cord and plug

Light bulb: since this lamp does not have a shade,
I opted for an Edison-style 40-watt light bulb – check
out your lamp kit for bulb requirements to make sure
you are in compliance

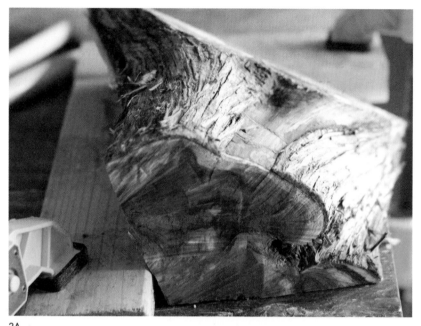

2A

2B

3

PREPARING THE WOOD

1 Look at the shape of the wood you are using and plan out where where you will insert the lamp socket for the bulb. In this example, the light bulb will be inserted in the middle of the wood at the wide end of the log. Saw the base flat if necessary to make sure that the finished lamp will not wobble.

2 No matter the shape of your wood, it will need to be secured before carving. Make sure you clamp it safely. Clamping a log such as this one to a table would not be prudent, so I made a jig to enclose it safely by clamping two scrap 2×4s to the table in an L shape, with the log set snugly inside. Use a chisel and mallet to take off the bark if you are using green wood.

CARVING THE LAMP

3 My aim with this project was to create a lamp that looks like an art sculpture, so I used a gouge to add some unique texture to the wood. Use the wood's natural shape and your own design ideas to guide you.

4 In this example, the light bulb will go in the middle of the wood, so an area of wood needs to be carved away to accommodate the bulb. Draw guidelines to indicate any areas of wood

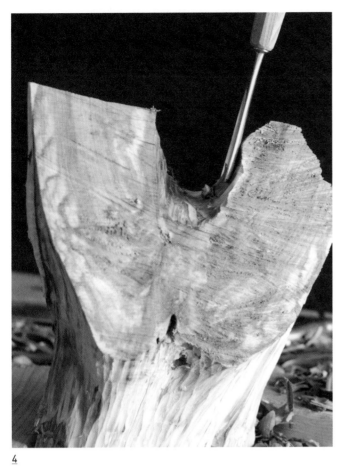

4

5

you need to remove from your piece. You can also use a handsaw to saw lines marking the outer edges of the wood to be removed. Setting boundaries with saw marks makes it easier to carve out the excess wood. I used a chisel and then a gouge to carve out the recess for the bulb.

5 As this wooden lamp started to take shape, it began looking more and more like a giant ham; cedar has rich reds and yellows, similar to a thick slice of bacon. I wanted this lamp to look like a fine art sculpture, not an ode to deli meat, so I decided to add more abstract texture to the front with the gouge.

6 Once the basic shape has been carved, use a spade bit to drill a hole for the lamp socket. I wanted the socket to be hidden, so I drilled a hole approximately 10cm (4in) deep and 3cm (1¼in) wide. You will need to adjust these measurements to suit the lamp kit you are using. The socket should fit snugly into the wood. I used a 25mm spade bit and then a gouge to carve around the drilled hole to make it 3cm (1¼in) wide. I could easily have used a larger spade bit, but did not want to risk the hole being too big, causing the socket to wobble in place.

6

7

10

7 The wire will need an exit point from the socket hole. On the back of the lamp, measure at least 4cm (1½in) south of the socket hole and drill an exit hole for the wire. The size of the exit hole will depend on your lamp kit. If your lamp kit needs assembly, you can simply feed the wire through the exit hole before you connect it to the socket and plug. My lamp kit came assembled, so I made the exit hole 2.5cm (1in) wide to fit the end of the plug through.

SANDING

8 If you are using green wood, put the piece outside to dry for a few days. During the drying process, the grain should start to rise slightly, priming it for sanding. If part of your lamp has delicate or thin carvings, you may want to let it sit outside for a few weeks, or even months, to dry out completely before sanding. When ready, sand the wood to your liking. Some parts of this lamp have been sanded all the way up to 400 grit, while the raw texture has been retained on other parts to contribute to a natural look.

FINISHING AND ASSEMBLY

9 Insert the lamp kit and test out the lamp by screwing in a light bulb. Assess whether there are any pieces of wood too close to the bulb. If so, take out the bulb and carve the wood away to create a larger gap between the wood and the bulb. Do not have the bulb too close to anything that can cause it to overheat.

10 If you want to use a finish, disassemble the lamp kit, remove all dust from the wood and apply your chosen finish. This lamp has been finished with teak oil to bring out the natural, rich colours of cedar. Reassemble the lamp kit and insert the bulb. A 40-watt tungsten filament bulb is used here because it requires low energy and gives off a soft, warm glow. Consult your lamp kit to see what type of bulb you should use.

—

'For this lamp I used a large chunk of cedar cut fresh from a neighbour's garden. Green wood is very easy to carve, but the final shape can sometimes warp as it dries out over time.'

CHAIN PLANT HOLDER

———

Carving a chain is a serious challenge, and while this practical project can serve as a small shelf, its true purpose is to impress your houseguests with your savvy woodworking skills.

YOU WILL NEED

Softwood or hardwood: 30 × 7.5cm (12 × 3in) and 7.5cm (3in) thick; American sycamore was used here

Pencil

Clamps

Mallet

#8 sweep gouge, 18mm

#9 sweep palm gouge, 5mm

#1s sweep double-bevel skew chisel, 16mm

Basic chip carving knife and/or #6 chip carving knife

Drill and 6mm and 5mm drill bits

Bandsaw or handsaw

Sandpaper: coarse (60-100 grit), medium (120-150 grit) and fine (220 grit)

Polyurethane, stain or finishing oil: mineral oil was used here

Lint-free cloth for finishing oil, or foam brush or paintbrush for polyurethane or stain

———

Templates: page 141

'This carving was made from American sycamore, which is light in colour with dark red "freckles". This hardwood has grain and texture similar to maple.'

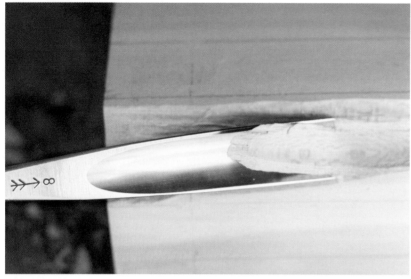

2

PREPARING THE WOOD

1 Use a pencil to mark a 2.5cm (1in) wide strip running along the centre of each face of the wood. Carry these lines across the end grain of the wood, so that each end of the block is divided into nine squares, forming a 2.5cm (1in) wide cross in the middle. Measure 2.5cm (1in) up from the bottom and draw a line around the block; this will form the shelf.

2 Clamp the wood to the table. Use a #8 gouge and mallet to take out the corners along the length of the wood, as far as the marked shelf line. The chips should be long and thin.

3 Line up a chisel on one of the marked lines running along the face of the wood and use the mallet to apply force to the blade. This will give you a straighter cut into the wood. Continue using a combination of the gouge and chisel to 'cut out' the cross shape. Remember to leave the shelf area intact.

3A

3B

4 Use the templates to sketch the chain links onto the cross of wood. The wood will now be a roughly cut 3D cross (with a shelf at one end) instead of a flat surface, so directly transferring a drawing of the complete chain would be tricky. You should therefore use the templates merely as a guide for how to sketch the outline of each link onto the wood. You can cut out the half-link template and place it onto the wood in the required positions to trace, or sketch out the links freehand in a similar fashion. Make sure that you draw the 'edge view' of the links on the outside edges of the cross, and the 'side view' of the links in the cutout corners. Each link is roughly 10cm (4in) long and 7.5cm (3in) wide. Note that the curved ends of the links should not be touching, so leave at least 2cm (¾in) between them. You should be able to fit three full links, plus a half link just below the shelf.

4A

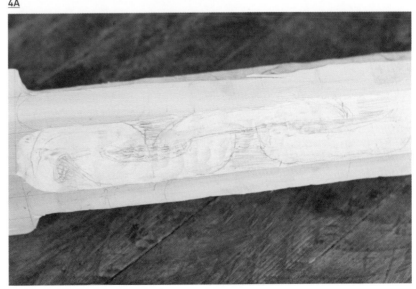

4B

5

5 Use a bandsaw or handsaw to cut out wedges of wood at the curved ends of the links. The overall shape of the links should now be much clearer.

CARVING THE LINKS

6 Use the shelf area to clamp the wood to the table. Reposition and reclamp the wood as necessary as you carve around each link. Working on one link at a time, use a 6mm bit to drill a few holes where the link needs to be

6A

6B

6D

separated from its neighbours. The holes serve as guides for where you need to carve away the wood. Use a #9 palm gouge to remove the rest of the wood, working all the way around the link until the wood has been separated before moving on to the next link.

6C

6E

8

9

10

11

7 Continue using the palm gouge to separate all the links. Starting out with thick links is advantageous when you have to carve tight areas – you can always make the links thinner, but you cannot add more wood once it has been carved away.

8 Use a chip carving knife to clean up the inner and outer areas of the links. All major signs of the palm gouge should disappear.

SANDING

9 Starting with 60-grit sandpaper, sand all of the links. Round out the corners and edges of each link. Continue sanding, moving up through the grits; I used 80, 150 and 220 grit.

MAKING THE SHELF

10 Choose which side will form the back of the shelf that affixes to the wall. Measure 13mm (½in) from the end of the block and mark a line around the front and both sides of the shelf. Measure 13mm (½in) from the back of the shelf and mark this point across the end grain and two sides of the shelf.

11 Use a bandsaw or handsaw to cut out the marked area to leave an L-shaped shelf. Use a 5mm bit to drill two holes to serve as nail holes for hanging the chain on a wall.

FINISHING

12 Finish sanding the entire chain and shelf with 220-grit sandpaper. Remove all dust and apply the finish of your choice. I used mineral oil.

CHAPTER 5

TEMPLATES

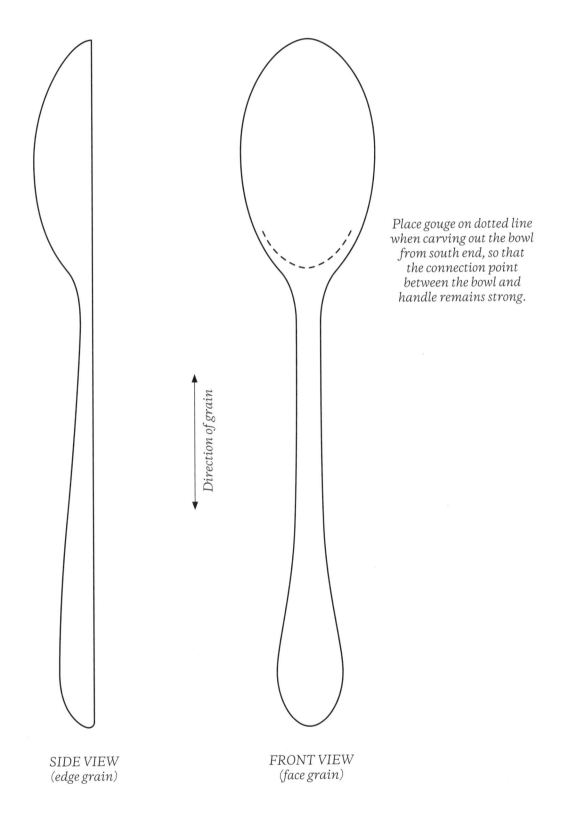

Place gouge on dotted line
when carving out the bowl
from south end, so that
the connection point
between the bowl and
handle remains strong.

Direction of grain

SIDE VIEW
(edge grain)

FRONT VIEW
(face grain)

SCOOP PAGE 60

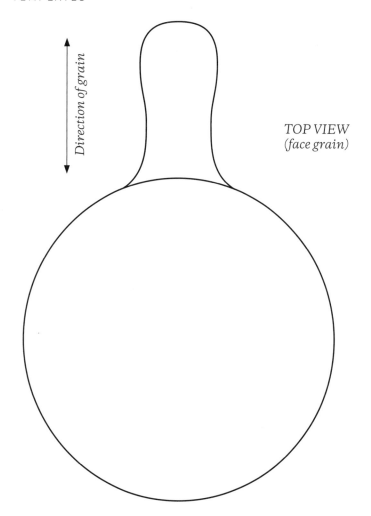

Direction of grain

TOP VIEW
(face grain)

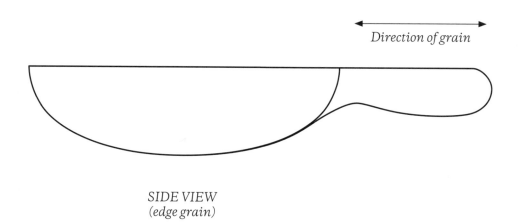

Direction of grain

SIDE VIEW
(edge grain)

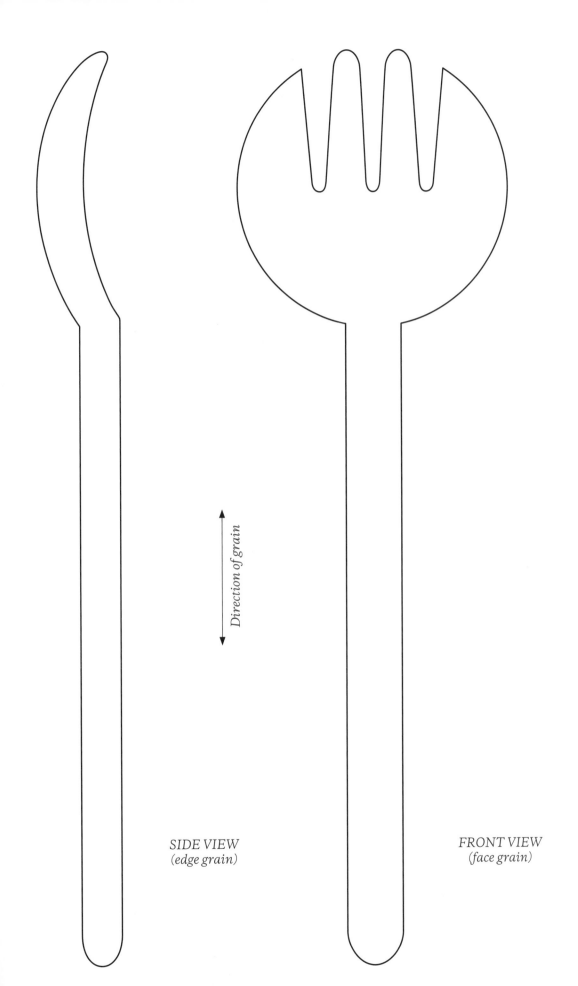

Direction of grain

SIDE VIEW
(edge grain)

FRONT VIEW
(face grain)

JAM SPREADRE PAGE 84

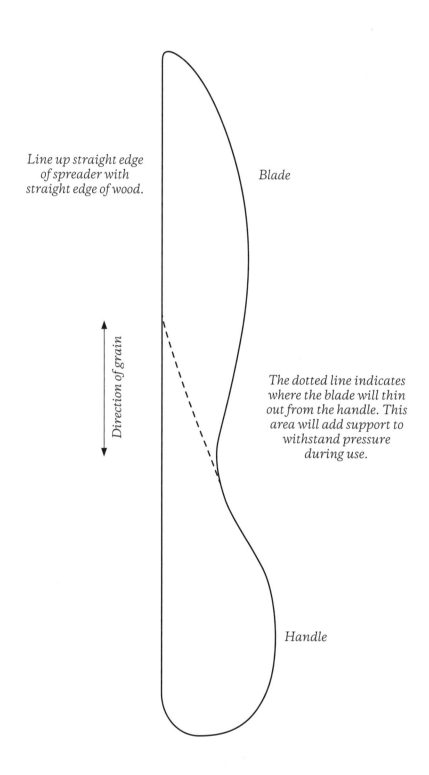

Line up straight edge of spreader with straight edge of wood.

Blade

Direction of grain

The dotted line indicates where the blade will thin out from the handle. This area will add support to withstand pressure during use.

Handle

SIDE VIEW
(face grain)

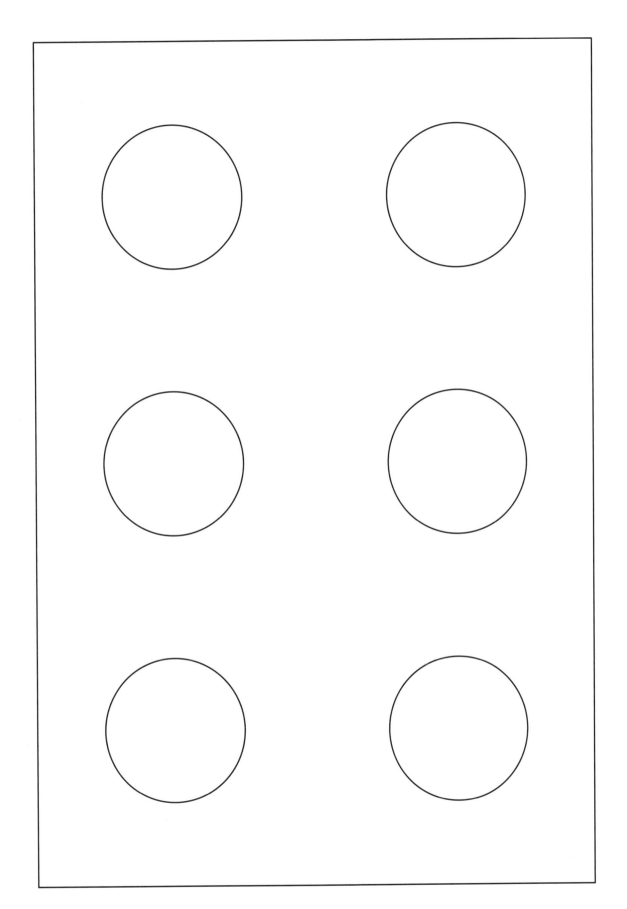

TOP VIEW
(face grain)

DOG BUSINESS CARD HOLDER PAGE 98

SIDE VIEW
(face grain)

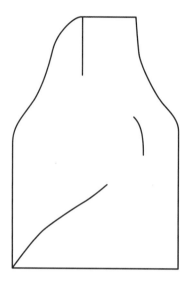

TOP AND BOTTOM VIEW
(face grain)

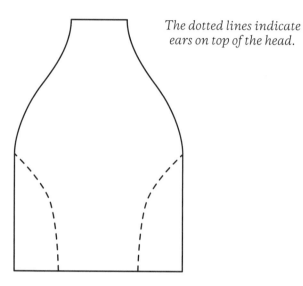

*The dotted lines indicate
ears on top of the head.*

*Carve deepest in
the corners.*

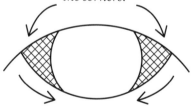

*Gradually carve
away wood
underneath the eye.*

HOW TO CARVE
A SIMPLE EYE
(enlarged detail)

TOP OF SNOUT
(end grain)

*The circle is drawn
larger than the
finished snout to allow
room for sanding.*

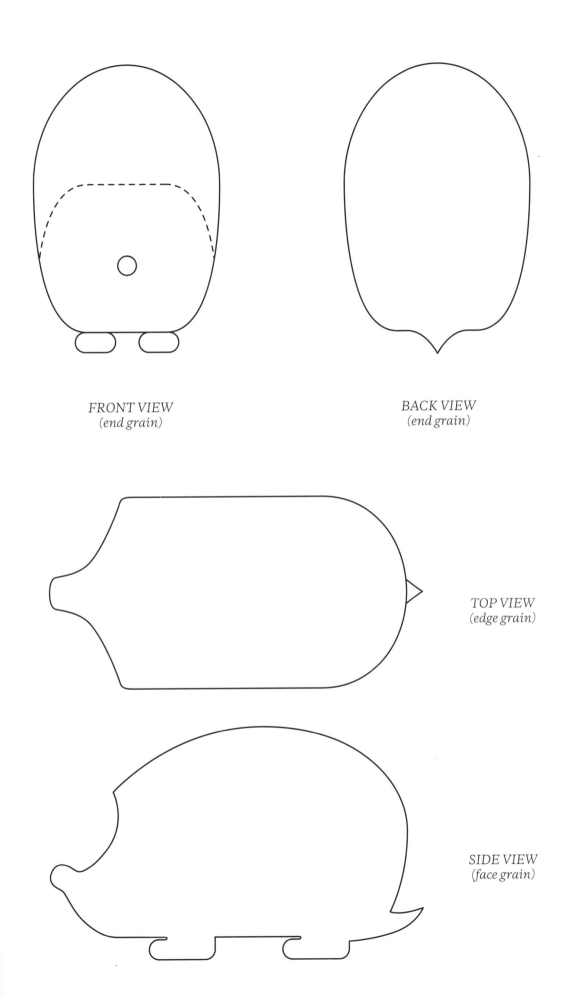

FRONT VIEW
(end grain)

BACK VIEW
(end grain)

TOP VIEW
(edge grain)

SIDE VIEW
(face grain)

COMB PAGE 112

DECORATIVE MOTIFS
*Choose and arrange motifs
on handle in any design you
like, or omit altogether.*

COMB
(face grain)

Direction of grain

CHAIN PLANT HOLDER PAGE 124

Shelf
Leave at least 2cm (¾in)
space between links.
3D VIEW

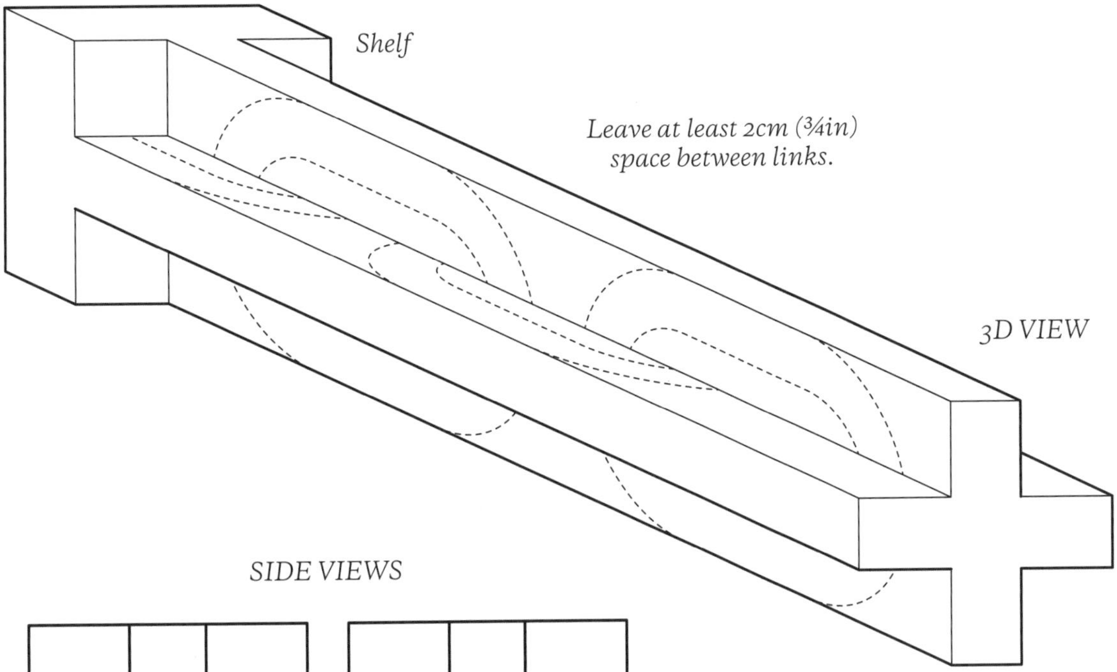

SIDE VIEWS

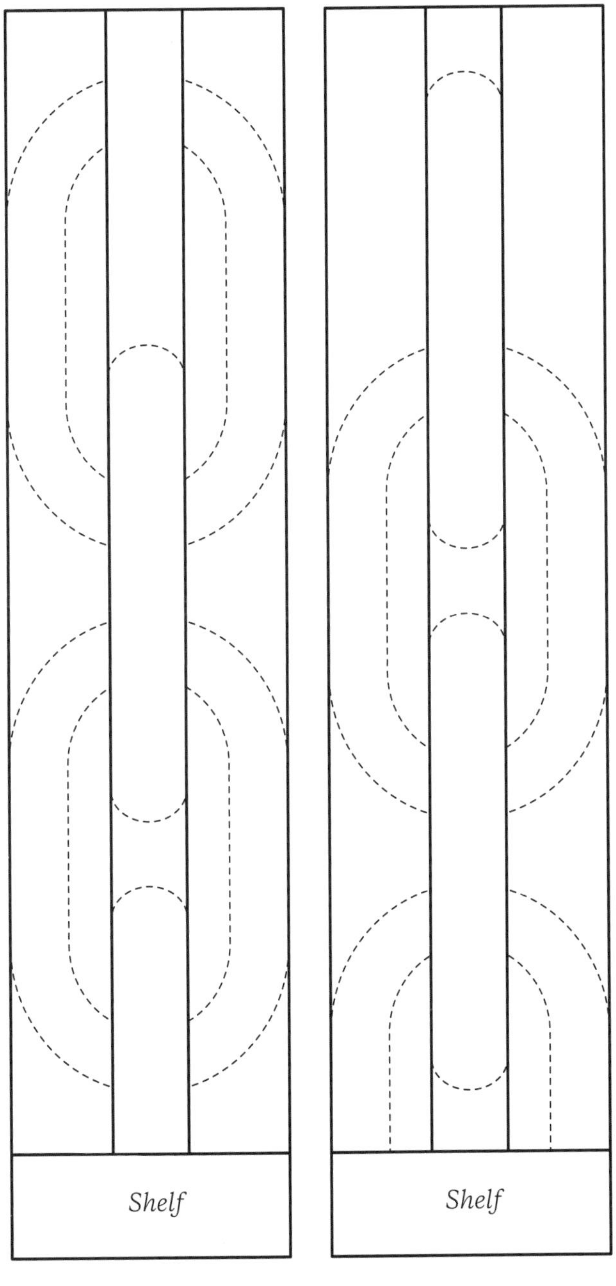

Shelf
Shelf

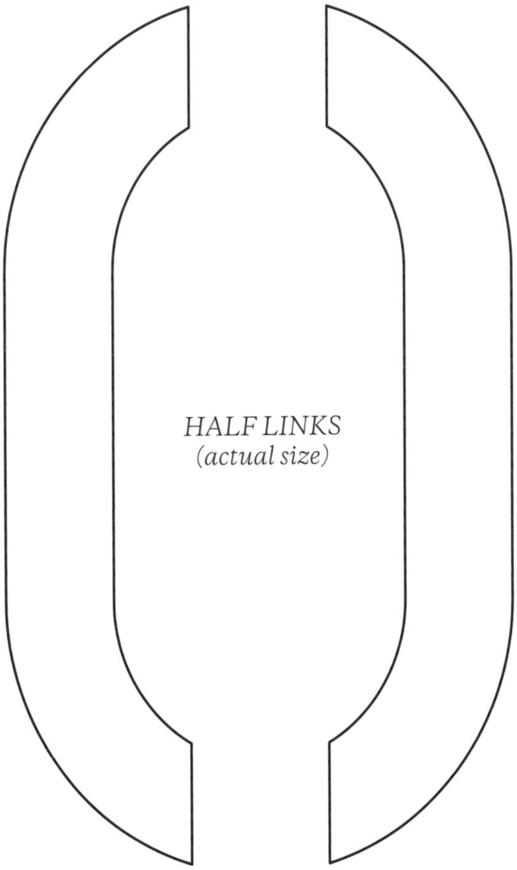

HALF LINKS
(actual size)

INDEX

CREDITS

———

AUTHOR'S ACKNOWLEDGEMENTS

A special thanks to Quarto Publishing, their patient editors and talented art directors, without whom this book would not have been possible.

I am very grateful for my roommates - John, Kristen, Liliana and Jen - who have been very supportive of my passion for woodworking, allowing me to work out of the studio in our home, despite the constant tool tinkering I engage in through all hours of the day.

Thank you to Ryan Rose, a talented Austin photographer, who was able to take a few photos for this book in a pinch.

And finally, to my mother, who when I was 20 years old, bought not one but two horses, and brought them home before she knew what to do with them. Now an accomplished equestrian, my mother taught me that the only prerequisite for achieving something, against all odds, is pure determination.

To those, at any age, wishing to embark on something unfamiliar, learn a new skill, develop a fresh talent or become a new person altogether, I hope this book inspires just that. And to know that nothing stands in your way so long as you remember that pure grit, courage and stubbornness will aid you in achieving the same.

Roll up thy sleeves,
Dive in.